CONTEMPLATING NOW

By the same author:
WITH LOVE TO THE CHURCH
TRAVELLING IN

CONTEMPLATING NOW

by
Monica Furlong

THE WESTMINSTER PRESS
PHILADELPHIA

Library of Congress Cataloging in Publication Data

Furlong, Monica.
  Contemplating now.

  1. Contemplation. I. Title.
BV5091.C7F87   1972   248'.3   72-2912
ISBN 0-664-24960-4

Foreword

'One who knows does not speak; one who speaks does not know,' says Lao Tzu, putting those who attempt to talk about contemplation firmly in their places. The dangers of talking pretentious rubbish in this field are great; the chance of having wise and useful things to say is slight. Those who 'know', know their own absurdity in trying to put the unspeakable into words and find the prospect too awesomely ludicrous to be undertaken at all. In any case, they have discovered how easily their listeners can abuse the truths of contemplation, either trying to capture their fluidity within some rigid system, or mistaking them for the clichés which they often resemble. Talking cannot achieve much in establishing these truths; it is only experience which fills them out, like a wind filling a sail, until life becomes directed and meaningful. And then there is little need to talk about it. It just needs to be lived.

Those who 'speak' are in a different case, and since I have 'spoken' in this book I feel the need to justify the attempt. One often speaks, it seems to me, not so much of what one has fully experienced but of what one longs for. I don't 'know' about the contemplative way of life, especially as it must be worked out in a secular environment, but I have a need to think and talk about its importance for me and for others, and a wish to discover how others think about it. I am not attempting to instruct, nor asking to be instructed; we live at a time in which ideas on this subject are in a state of confusion, and in which those who think they know most about it often know least. Instruction may come to us in the most unlikely places, and from the most unlikely people, and we need only to be simple and flexible enough to accept it when it comes. All I am trying to do is share what I am thinking and experimenting with, partly in the hope that I myself will listen to my own plea for stillness, partly in the hope that others will feel like sharing their own experience of stillness with me. The few who are really qualified to talk (instruct) in this field are not likely to write books about it, but all the more reason that those of us who long for their wisdom and integrity should share our own stumbling attempts to follow them. I hope it can be done without pretension.

It is perhaps important to mention that I have taken liberties with the definition of the word 'contemplation'. Among Christians it is sometimes used in a particular technical way, as describing the stage of mystical experience known as the 'illuminative way', a stage which often succeeds the 'purgative way', and precedes the 'unitive way' or 'spiritual marriage'. In the course of the illuminative way verbal and meditative forms of prayer give way to a wordless form of prayer. Although I have made use of the latter idea, I have in general used the word contemplation in a much wider sense, closer to the Eastern way of thinking about religious experience, and touching upon many aspects of life which are not overtly religious at all. I should like to think that the book is not about religion (religion being only the metaphor with which we struggle to talk about human experience), but about life.

Contents

Preparation

Contemplation

To WRITE ABOUT contemplation is to explore an area of human consciousness which has been trodden by genius. It is not the kind of human genius which, in recent times, has moved or interested us greatly. Our sympathy and admiration goes more easily and fashionably to other kinds of genius – we pay lip service readily to Mozart or Shakespeare but not to St. John of the Cross or Julian of Norwich or Lao Tzu. On the surface of it this is reasonable enough. The pleasure that we may get from a Mozart Mass or a performance of *Hamlet* is more evident than that we may get from a reading of the mystics. In all cases what we are dealing with is reflection upon the experience of human life and emotion, but the further the reflection moves from the ordinary experience of ordinary men, as in the case of St. John's poems, then the less easily will it seem to speak to us.

When St. John writes of the peculiar suffering of the man who tries to know God there will probably be few who recognise the experience. 'Just as, the clearer is the light, the more it blinds and darkens the pupils of the owl, the more directly we look at the sun, the greater is the darkness which it causes in our visual faculty overcoming and overwhelming it through its own weakness.'[1]

Perhaps we need to recognise such mystics as explorers. Like the man who is the first to cross a desert the mystic has a kind of symbolic importance for us. We may never have the least intention of crossing the same desert ourselves, we may not even be intensely interested in the minutiae of his journey, but somehow the quality of life is changed by the fact that *he* has crossed it. He has shown us something about the potentiality of the world about us – we shall know things about it that we did not know before. And equally he has shown us something about the potentiality of a human being – that to be a human being includes courage which, in turn, implies a certain trust in the ordering of the world. An affirmation.

I am interested in the affirmation of the mystics because I think that exposure to them, like exposure to the explorer, the composer, the poet, deepens the quality of life. It is *our* world he writes about even if we never see the territory he describes, and the kind of courage with which he makes his journey is a kind that we recognise, in germ, within ourselves. Atheist, agnostic, or believer in one religion or another, godseeking is built into us and we cannot be totally indifferent to others' success, nor the emotions which it produces in us. We live in a period in which men have become embarrassed by this aspect of human feeling, really because of new and profound difficulties about the person of God, but despite the difficulty religious emotion does not simply go away. It may suffer

1. *Noche Oscura II*, St. John of the Cross, tr. E. Allison Peers, O.U.P.

repression or it may emerge, violently, in unexpected Dionysian bursts, or it may (though in fewer and fewer cases) take the path of traditional piety, but for those of us whom none of these answers quite fits (though we may need one or more of them at some stage of our development) there is the problem of how to care for and nourish the religious side of our natures.

How does one live with religious emotion in the twentieth century? The longing for meaning, for wholeness, and for what the French philosopher Hubert Benoit calls 'inner work' is common to everybody, but no one, any longer, is sure of what the 'work' consists of. Is it a matter of learning meditation from the Maharishi or taking LSD? A question of turning to psycho-analysis, or returning to the Christian Church? Does it need a vocabulary of sin, repentance, forgiveness, love, or of trauma, repression, acceptance, transference? Is prayer a method, or do chemicals do it better? How much fulfilment do we need on a simple level of sexual happiness, worldly acceptance, and success in achievement to make a realistic assessment of our own value? And how far does that kind of fulfilment prevent us, as by a drug, from perceiving the strange ambiguity hidden in our desires, so that fulfilment, at the ordinary level, carries a disappointment which it is no longer fashionable to voice?

I want to try to struggle with these problems. They could be discussed in many different frameworks and under many headings. I propose to discuss them in the dress of contemplation – the word men have used, in the West, to describe man's struggle to become still enough to reflect the face of God, or, in the East, the effort (or non-effort) to live fully in the present moment.

Saint and Sinner

In England, in the Middle Ages, many a village had its own hermit, just as it had its own idiot, its own drunkard, its own prostitute. In a small community, as in the groups with which people experiment nowadays, each had his own clearly defined role, partly defined by his own character, partly forced upon him by the others. In a sense it was a grave limitation – to be condemned for life to play the bad woman (or the holy woman) for others. It left part of the personality permanently fallow. But in another sense the village community offered total fulfilment. Because you lived cheek by jowl with human extremes you could *together* achieve a sort of wholeness; there was always someone there to do the bits you couldn't do, to let you live vicariously in their goodness or badness.

Urban development brought about a very different state of affairs. No one who lives in a town can know all the other people who live there, and even when he knows a good many it will not be in the close, cradle-to-the-grave way that the villager knows those about him. Here and there he will find others who remind him of the undeveloped sides of his personality, but if the community is large enough, and impersonal enough, he may have too little knowledge of his neighbours for that kind of fulfilment. In turn, they know nothing of him and of the way he would appear in a close community where he had nothing to hide.

Loss of such interaction makes men feel a disappointment and sense of loss which may express itself in a spectrum of emotion which ranges from mild dissatisfaction with life to intense loneliness, neuroticism, suicidal tendencies, and possibly, madness. In our own time many are struggling to fight the problem with groups — group therapy, group dynamics, groups for widows, the divorced, for parents of handicapped children, for alcoholics, and gamblers, discussion groups, prayer groups, and many more. In the group there is a giving of the self which thus paradoxically gains an identity. This looks like the best answer we have yet found for the loneliness and inner poverty of urban man.

Yet what of those for whom the group does not seem to provide what they need? For some, solitude with all its pains is as much a necessity as the group is for others. I am not here talking about the solitude which springs from neurotic difficulties in relationship. Obviously, either an excessive taste for solitude, or excessive gregariousness may be rooted in neurosis, and it may well be neurosis which, initially, forms in us a taste for one thing or the other. I am, however, assuming a real attempt to be done with neurotic choices, which means, for each of us, trying to adjust the balance of our personality. For the gregarious this means a courageous moving into solitude. For those to whom loneliness feels the natural state, it means attempting deeper relationship.

Yet when the necessary 'inner work' of correcting the balance has been done we are still primarily gregarious or lonely; when we have discovered, painfully, the extent of our neurosis and learned to allow for it, we shall probably return to our original path.

✓ The contemplative is primarily the man of solitude, and the question for him is how he can achieve the wholeness of living which others enjoy through partaking in the group. Where will he find all that he needs to form the pattern of life, i.e. good and bad, male and female, saint and sinner, the hermit and the village idiot. Answer, and this is the simple mystery of contemplation, inside himself. Each waits there for him, does not necessarily demand to be projected upon others in love or hate (though he needs to experience projection), can be discovered and contribute to his wholeness. There is nothing that he needs that is not already there. He carries his village within him.

Active and Passive

Busyness is an illusion. I do not mean that in particular situations there are not pressing practical tasks which need to be done. I mean that, far more than most of us are prepared to acknowledge, we choose excessive busyness, actually organise it for ourselves. It anaesthetises the feelings of inadequacy and insignificance which assail us when we admit that we have remarkably little to do.

We are very good at deceiving ourselves. For example, the doctor, social worker, clergyman may arrange his life in such a way that needy people never cease to come to him. They take a huge toll of his physical and mental strength, they invade, or perhaps destroy, his private life. He is a man who needs to be needed, and who is probably afraid of rejecting others' needs. So he works to the edge of physical or mental collapse. If he is lucky his unconscious will arrange for him conveniently spaced illnesses so that his exhausted body and mind can recover themselves without his ever needing to come to grips with the basic problem. If he is unlucky the first illness may be a disabling one, a heart attack or stroke which places himself in the category of the needy. In fact, of course, he was always needy, needing his patients or clients or parishioners, as much as they needed him.

Women organise their busyness rather differently. In some cases they time child-bearing in such a way as to forbid themselves an escape from busyness. But more often they make themselves prisoners to domesticity and the family, setting themselves ever higher standards of housekeeping, insisting on ever more unrealistic standards of duty and helpfulness to those around them. Again, illness is a blessed escape.

A lot of the difficulty in all this is that we have grown up in a society that assumes that activity is virtuous and passivity is wicked. 'Satan,' the Victorians liked to say, 'finds mischief for idle hands to do.' We want to be good, we want to be the sort of person that society admires and approves, and of whom we ourselves can approve. To this end we work ceaselessly, 'good' children who understand what is demanded of them in a particular rigid framework and who are afraid if the framework is taken away or even criticised. We can only relax when we have done our stint; we may not sit down after dinner until we have done the washing-up.

Activity has obvious advantages. Like Mussolini, it makes the trains run, more or less, on time. It keeps us clean, punctual, obedient. It gets things done, and when one looks at the squalor and corruption of an Eastern city like Calcutta, or even at the grubbiness and social inadequacy of many a hippie, then activity seems not at all a bad idea.

There are two difficulties about activity, though. One is that busyness breeds busyness. It is not only that if we are surrounded by busy people then idleness, however fruitful, becomes difficult to maintain. It is that busyness, like a taste for sugar, becomes an addiction. We discover that we can squeeze more and more work out of ourselves (the more we do so the more approving others tend to be), that it becomes harder to stop, and that when we do stop we find it difficult to enjoy ourselves. Holidays make us feel guilty and must be paid for with a spell of overwork before and after to placate the two fiercest gods of our society — work and money. Since nearly everyone around us worships these gods there is no one to protest at what is happening to us (except perhaps children who have a different sense of priorities). Only our bodies protest. They ache, irritate, ulcerate, form addictions, grow obese, thrombose and haemorrhage in dumb revenge. We do not have much respect for our bodies and we respond to their demands grudgingly, if at all, as to the complainings of a morose and difficult spouse.

The other difficulty about activity is that sooner or later we have to look and see what all our busyness is in aid of and this tends to be a disillusioning experience; so much of our sweat, toil, tears and blood squandered and remarkably little to show for it. We look back at our lives and are amazed at the triviality of achievements which once seemed so important. And so much of our effort seems misdirected, and unnecessarily frenetic. We are bound to make mistakes — it is part of growing up, part of growing. In the first half of our lives, in particular, we need our activity to discover the world and our own place in it. Yet as we grow towards middle age busyness tends to be less a necessity to establish our place in the world, or even to cope with the place that we have, than a nervous habit which we find it hard to control. Work is not so much fulfilment or hard necessity as a tic.

Drilled as we are in the idea that work is the supreme virtue, then if we refuse it we feel unworthy, depressed, and frightened. The retired easily feel unwanted and inferior. Life without the habit of industry appears drained of all colour (especially if we have also tended to repress the aesthetic, religious, and emotional sides of ourselves), a futile gift which we must drag out, like a wounded worm, to the grave. Only occasionally does it occur to us that we continue to arrange our lives in a work-perpetuating way, while never ceasing to complain of our intolerable busyness.

We rarely see the absurdity of this. The principal absurdity is that each of us is capable of only so much work before our health suffers and our efficiency is impaired. We can, by driving ourselves, achieve miracles of work on a particular day, but the quality and quantity of our work will be reduced on the subsequent day. If we force ourselves to overwork over a protracted period then there is a gradual slowing down, both mental and physical. It might even be possible to work out, for an individual, how many hours of work, how many hours of sleep, how many hours of relaxation, are necessary to produce a consistently high quality of work. But our basis for thinking about work tends to have moral overtones rather than physical or psychological ones.

The other absurdity is that activity is only worthwhile if its goals and methods have been carefully thought out beforehand. The more personally or socially significant the activity, the greater the depth of reflection needed, and in many cases, if not all, reflection seems to demand periods of idleness.

If overwork causes inefficiency (the inefficiency of bad health among other kinds), and a refusal to reflect produces misdirected or futile action, then an intelligent society would withhold praise from those who overwork themselves (perceiving the neurosis embedded in the activity).

What is the alternative to obsessive busyness? Not, in my view, obsessive idleness (which suggests a fear of life and an inability to lay hold of it). What we seem to have lost, but can still perceive in primitive peoples and in animals, is a sense of the rhythmic quality of life, activity alternating with passivity. What we tend to forget is that the swing from one mood to the other need not be a matter of conscious choice. If we live fully in our activity or passivity, and do not seek to shorten or prolong either state with drugs or a poultice of guilt, then before long we automatically seek its opposite. Brought up in a Western society, we find it difficult to relax our conscious interference with our bodies and minds. Having interfered so profoundly with our natural rhythms (the rhythms of breathing, sleeping, eating, to look no further) we live in a permanent condition of anxious mistiming.

'Do you know why you cannot wait for the shot and

why you get out of breath before it has come?' the
Japanese master of archery asks his European pupil.
'The right shot at the right moment does not come
because you do not let go of yourself . . . What stands
in your way is that you have a much too wilful will.
You think that what you do not do yourself does not
happen.' . . .

'What must I do then?' I asked thoughtfully.

'You must learn to wait properly.'[2]

To learn to wait is, for our overstrained bodies and
minds, the hardest thing. We do not really trust the world
around us, and think that if we are not constantly manipulating it disaster will overtake us. We apply ourselves (and
much of our activity) to manipulating the future in such a
way as to avoid the pains of the past, whether of failure,
loss, disappointment, accident, ridicule and scorn. It is
not unreasonable to try to avoid pain, but manipulation
(the success or failure of which sets up acute tension
within us) becomes a god in itself, demanding all our
attention, cutting us off not only from a degree of suffering
and discomfort, but also from unpredictable and spontaneous forms of happiness.

Passivity, and a non-manipulative attitude to life tend
to exist side by side.

Passivity

Passivity is receptive, containing, fertile, and finally,
productive. It is the feminine pole of human experience,
and neither a man nor a woman can be creative without it.

2. *Zen in the Art of Archery*, Eugen Herrigel, Routledge and
Kegan Paul.

Perhaps we despise it because it makes us feel helpless, and reminds us of the dependence of early childhood, when we were fed, bathed, carried and had little control over our own comfort or discomfort, or because it reminds us of old age when, as the Bible says, 'another shall gird thee, and carry thee whither thou wouldest not'.

Or perhaps we fear it because we fear being mentally seduced by the peace and inertia of the womb. This is a real danger. Contemplation demands a degree of cutting oneself off from external stimuli and when these are removed we can find ourselves tumbling into extreme lassitude, and surrendering to sleep.

Passivity is neither sleep nor lassitude; it is what the Zen masters call a 'purposeless tension'. It is like the surface tension of a pool of water, or the tension of a string on an instrument which is not yet being played. It is flexible and ready, reflecting as the pool reflects the sky.

The question is, why should we bother? The kind of passivity I am talking about is a costly achievement for a human being, and it is ludicrous that it has often been discussed as a duty to a god who is so dimly known. What each of us wants to know before labouring up such a difficult mountain is 'What do I get out of it?'

I believe that we shouldn't bother if we can help ourselves. If we can resist then it is probably right for us to do so. It isn't a duty. If it happens at all it's an addiction, akin perhaps to an addiction to writing or painting. It is an attempt to establish unity between oneself and the world about one. Having let the original womb go (with so much suffering) it is an acknowledgment that the world itself is to be trusted as the womb was trusted.

Solitude — 1

Solitude is the real nub of the contemplative experience. Those who are drawn to contemplation feel a strong attraction to solitude; they feel sad, sick, increasingly desperate unless they can arrange their lives in such a way that periods of solitude occur frequently. They are not necessarily introverted people, though many are. Some contemplatives say that it is only early in the development of a contemplative that prolonged solitude is really essential — that given practice it is possible to develop an interior solitude even in the most noisy and demanding surroundings. But they would probably agree that without the initial experience of solitude, and the chance to learn its advantages and disadvantages, most contemplatives would never get any further. For the contemplative, solitude represents the heart's desire, or rather the conditions under which to achieve the heart's desire, and he needs what one might call the 'disillusioning fulfilment' of it, as others need the disillusioning fulfilment of requited love.

A major difficulty for the contemplative, I believe, lies in distinguishing the pathological elements in his attraction to solitude and contemplative experience, and in trying to face these. If he suspects that there is in himself a fear of emotional or physical involvement, a dislike of the flesh, an unwillingness to be a fully human being with the whole equipment of appetites and desires proper to a human being, then he has got to do a lot of work before he can start on contemplation proper at all. He has got to cure himself of being an angel, and learn to love his humanness, and that of others, before he can love God.

Others, however, do not have this problem, but the opposite one. Knowing themselves to be all too human, and fearing the consequences of this, they feel they can bury the whole problem by turning their back on it and loving God instead. I don't think this will do either. We've got to discover God in and through being who we are and not by pretending to be somebody else. Wherever we start there must be a patient and perpetual effort to observe in ourselves tendencies towards self-deception, towards neurotic escape. This means reading the books, and keeping in touch with the people, who are going to ask the hard questions and listening albeit impatiently to the criticisms of others. Whatever the degree of asceticism which belongs properly to contemplative experience, it is clear that by far the largest portion is needed in a certain astringency of intellectual approach. The contemplative must not only use his mind to dismantle his feelings, but also to induce and develop a self-mocking approach. This offers some small safeguard in an area of human experience which offers all too much scope for pretension and unreality.

The difficulty about solitude is that it heightens experience. It may therefore either speed the movement towards wholeness (if undertaken at the right stage in a person's human development), or encourage regression into pathological attitudes. This is why a lot of 'inner work' may be necessary before it is right, or safe, to explore the inner territory too far. Luckily, many people have a strong disinclination to explore until they are ready to do so, which must be respected. Equally, most people have some urge to move in the direction of contemplative experience, and it is important that they should go as far as they can.

Solitude – 2

The purpose of solitude is that, cut off from external stimuli, we shall be able to fix our attention in such a way as to achieve a different state of consciousness. I want to talk more about that state of consciousness farther on in the book. For the moment I want to talk more about the incidental experiences which occur in solitude.

One of the early experiences of those who try to fix their attention in a state of solitude is that of recurring sleep. They may not feel particularly tired to start with, and it may not be a time of day in which they are in the habit of sleeping, but with monotonous regularity they will find themselves dropping off to sleep. To begin with, it may be that they are more tired than they realised, and just as the first day or two of a holiday finds out our depth of accumulated tiredness, so the attempt at being non-active discovers a weariness that we scarcely knew about.

But that is far from being the full extent of the problem. Contemplatives, East and West, have to wrestle with the problem, at least in the earlier stages of solitude. The Buddhist habit of occasionally striking monks over the shoulder with a stick during prayer is sometimes said to be to keep the sleepers awake, though there are other explanations. Some Eastern Orthodox mystics describe a particular technique, a sort of psychic leap, in which the drowsy contemplative can move immediately into a state of attentiveness. Once the technique is mastered they claim that it is never again lost. Certainly drowsiness is a problem which tends to afflict apprentices more than others.

If we were to discuss the phenomenon in psychological terms we might say that it represented 'resistance'. The contemplative fears the experience he is about to meet, and he takes one of the few escape routes left open to him – he relapses into unconsciousness.

Another common experience in solitude which has much in common with sleepiness is boredom. The contemplative, deprived of the illusion of inner life which came to him as result of external stimuli, suffers a sense of deadness, of lassitude, almost of weakness, rather like the feeling of physical weakness which follows a severe illness. He feels as if he is falling apart, in a state of dangerous disintegration, and becomes increasingly desperate for something on which his mind can clutch. Like sleepiness I believe this is a mask for fear. Thomas Merton quotes the experience of one of the Desert Fathers going through precisely this painful struggle, as his mind tries to make sense of a landscape from which all the familiar landmarks have been removed. 'A brother asked one of the Elders saying: What shall I do, Father, for I work none of the works of a monk but here I am in torpor eating and drinking and sleeping and in bad thoughts and in plenty of trouble, going from one struggle to another and from thoughts to thoughts.'[3]

Akedia, it is said, is the sickness of monks, but to a lesser degree it is the sickness of all who decide to make the inner journey, since this demands the experiment of de-

3. 'The Cell', Thomas Merton, *Sobernost*, Series 5, No. 5 (Summer 1967).

all
1

priving oneself for periods of external stimuli. Merton points out the way in which the loss of stimuli threatens our sense of identity.

> Afflicted with boredom and hardly knowing what to do with himself the disciple represents to himself a more fruitful and familiar way of life, in which he appears to himself to 'be someone' and to have a fully recognisable and acceptable identity, a 'place in the Church', but the Elder tells him that his place in the Church will never be found by following these ideas and images of a plausible identity. Rather it is found by travelling in a way that is new and disconcerting because it has never been imagined by us before, or at least we have never conceived it as useful or even credible . . . A way in which we seem to lose our identity and become nothing.[4]

Sliding down the precipice into nothingness, his fingers clutching at crevices, it is not surprising if the contemplative is seized by panic, a panic which may take the form of sleep or *akedia*. He knows that he is losing the affirmation of his identity by others, an affirmation which to most, if not all, of us constitutes one of the major comforts of life. There is real pain in this loss, even though it is temporary, and in his pain he may regress and turn to childish forms of sensuality, pathetically trying to fill his emptiness in ways which bring him little real comfort or satisfaction. He feels sad and lonely, envious of the imagined joys of others. He experiences himself as the greatest of burdens. He becomes lazy and inattentive.

4. Ibid.

all

The terror of non-being is so fundamental to a human being that it takes exceptional courage and determination to undergo the contemplative experience, and it is one that is only possible in maturity. The cure for the panic is not to struggle and to clutch but to let go, actually to speed the descent into nothingness. The contemplative must let go not only of his fear and his corresponding attempt to control and manipulate his disturbing experience, but also of his own sick and regressed side. He must look dispassionately, and without contempt or shame upon the fantasies conjured by his mind in loneliness, since even wallowing in shame or self-disgust is the refusal to let go of his identity. He must let go. He longs to let go. He is terrified of letting go. He dare not let go. He cannot escape unless he does let go.

He has to live with his severe conflict with as much equanimity as he can manage. Merton's Elder replies to the brother, 'Just you stay in your cell and cope with all this as best you can without being disturbed by it,' and another Elder tells a young monk that his *akedia* is due to his having lost sight of what he calls the *akme*. The *akme*, says Merton, has both a temporal and a spatial implication: it is at once the 'real point' and the 'moment of truth'.

What is this real point or moment? It is the moment when the contemplative lets go. It is submission, self-giving, trusting (though none of these things are possible unless the conflict has been faithfully gone through). It is loss of identity. It is crucifixion. It is death.

This death or moment of truth achieves a transformation which is at the heart of the contemplative experience.

alf

In Merton's words, we discover that 'where we are is where we belong'. In mysterious fashion the pain and sense of loss when they have been fully experienced flower into new life. Pain becomes joy. Frustration becomes fulfilment. Death becomes resurrection. A sense of order and of harmony floods through all our emotions and all our actions. Fear, boredom, lassitude, sadness, loneliness vanish.

It is important to remember that though this experience is one more familiar to the contemplative than to most men, it is by no means an uncommon one among people who do not regard themselves as contemplative. Many people have had the experience in recovering from bereavement, illness, marital and other forms of conflict, or indeed most forms of severe pain. They are led to the puzzling discovery first that suffering and joy can become difficult to distinguish from one another, and then to the suspicion that they may turn out to be the same thing.

God

What hinders real religious discussion at the present time, I believe, is the widespread embarrassment over the word God. Like all embarrassment it has hidden roots. One fruitful source of embarrassment is that God is unverifiable, and because verification seems, at this stage of human development, the best way of controlling a difficult, and often dangerous environment, we are uneasy with what is unverifiable and with the side of ourselves which is all credulity. We despise the childish side of man which claims that what we would like to be true *is* true (and we remember Freud's criticism of religion on the grounds that it was a womb fantasy, a denial of the reality-principle).

There are other reasons for embarrassment, however, besides these. One is that belief in God, in the West, has until recently been so universal, so taken for granted, and so much the keystone of thought, culture, politics and morals that it took on a kind of corporate meaning which existed almost independently of what individual men and women actually experienced for themselves. Unless they were to find themselves disturbingly at odds with their culture then God was something or someone who must tacitly be taken for granted. The majority of people went easily along with this requirement (as nowadays they go along with equal ease with the requirement not to take God seriously), taking part in public forms of religious expression and carrying the beliefs and ideas drawn from these back into their social and moral lives. There is a peculiar comfort about taking part in group rites which has a self-perpetuating quality about it. Doubts about the point or meaning of the rites can be silenced with the thought that *everybody* does them, and the fact that *everybody* does them does in fact endow the rites with a vitality which is addictive. Thus religious ceremonies or beliefs become compulsive to the extent to which everybody does them or accepts them. (The unconscious realisation of which may have played a big part in some of the more brutal acts of Christian history – for example, the forcible conversion of the Jews, and the persecution of every kind of deviationist. We can watch the same pattern at work nowadays in the intense Soviet persecution of conflicting ideologies, however feeble the minorities involved.) They lose their healing power when they cease to be a group experience.

The 'ordinary man' is then caught in a cruel dilemma. He has been brought up in an environment which has taught him that belief in God is something he'd be wise to take for granted. He has gone through the outward motions of this belief, i.e. got married in church, had his children baptised, perhaps been confirmed or had his children confirmed without asking too many rebellious questions about it all. Knowing that underneath little of

34

it really touched him, he has avoided discussion of God for fear his sham would be exposed. He is embarrassed because life has forced him to live a lie, but he is more embarrassed now, when the voices which proclaim it a lie are so numerous, than he was a hundred years ago when only a select few dared to say so.

A different kind of embarrassment may afflict the kind of man or woman who draws security in life not from the sense that he or she belongs to the consenting mass of mankind but from the sense that they are 'different'. Whatever the mass admire they tend to dislike and whatever the mass despise they will look kindly upon. It is an innocent kind of sham as the 'ordinary man's' kind of sham is innocent – an understandable shift to keep going in a destructive world. But since belief as well as doubt may overwhelm men (in the form of some kind of experience whose authenticity they cannot doubt without doubting their own sanity), such people may find themselves profoundly affected by numinous experience while their public stance is one of scorn and scepticism allowing no vocabulary for the inner truth.

Embarrassment afflicts people who dare not admit their real feelings for fear of the hostility or scorn they might arouse. And so where God is concerned many people play a double game, a game which may acquire additional nuances from their unwillingness to ally themselves openly with the kind of people who *are* believers, or with the kind of people who publicly doubt.

Not everyone is embarrassed, however. Fortunately there have always been people who were not content with conventional belief or disbelief but who needed to work out something about God for themselves. Their relation to organised religion has been an ambiguous one. They have sometimes been within the Church, pursuing their researches for the most part within her framework even when at odds with others. And they have sometimes been outside the Church, at best tolerated by her and at worst persecuted.

Seekers who could not take God on hearsay had one clear course open to them – they must discover how to experience God for themselves. Therefore, by every means open to them – asceticism and prayer, love of their fellow-men, intellectual activity, art, physical love and drugs (though Christianity has rather eschewed the last two) they have pursued the knowledge of God. Organised religion has played an interesting and on the whole, I believe, salutary part in their research, though it has been misunderstood because the psychological role of the Church has been misunderstood.

It has been customary to talk as if the purpose of the Church has been to put people in touch with God, or to keep them in touch with God. But although on the face of it it seems to exist to help its adherents into relationship with God, it equally, and perhaps essentially, plays the opposite role of trying to filter out an experience of transcendence which might be overwhelming. A highly developed liturgy such as the Roman Mass can be seen as the tracing out in drama of a reality which the participants could not bear to experience too often, yet which they wish to be kept in touch with.

Both individuals and communities may need to keep a certain balance between, on the one hand, mystical experiences so powerful that they are a threat to sanity, and on the other, life devoid of any deep inner experience. History suggests that men have a need to swing to and fro between these two extremes.

The Church's role has, therefore, it seems to me, been one of helping to maintain a certain balance between mystical experience and 'ordinary' life, a real contribution to sanity. It has also, until recently, offered a strong interpretative contribution – whatever a man was going through he could make approximate sense of it within the existing framework (or he could work out his own position by denying the Church's interpretation).

The godseeker's role, however, has been a more straightforward one, and it has inevitably led sometimes into conflict with the Church. The godseeker is less concerned with sanity (though it is important that others are concerned for him) and he has to take risks with balance if he is to make any progress at all.

If we are to get through the embarrassment which inhibits discussion of the area of experience usually described as God, and remain sympathetic to, or anyhow tolerant of, the godseeker whose primary need is to experience, then it seems we must explore new ways (or old ways that we have forgotten) of talking about God, which release our real feelings.

One of the difficulties is what Mircea Eliade calls the 'provincialism' of Christianity. Those in our society who still have a language, albeit a dying language, for talking about religious experience, find difficulty in believing that there are other, highly developed languages which may be equally effective. It's as if a Frenchman should refuse to believe that German really was a language. So pervasive is this attitude of mind that it may be necessary for those whose primary religious nourishment has been Christian to immerse themselves in another form of religion in order to correct the mental malformation.

For the majority of men nowadays, however, this problem does not arise. They do not have an effective language, not even a Christian one, in which to talk about religious experience, and to the extent to which language enables experience, they are deprived men.

I believe that a way out of this state (which affects us all to some degree) may be to learn, or re-learn, something about *playing* with the idea of God, as children learning to talk play with words and sounds. What follows is a sort of playing — idle, random ways of coming at the idea of God.

We can afford randomness since God (and religion) are metaphors for something for which we have no words and which we cannot adequately describe. We make quick verbal sketches and put the word God to them — God the father, son or Holy Ghost, God the king, God the judge, God the lover, God (according to Julian of Norwich) the tender mother. Outside the Judaeo-Christian tradition the sketches become different. The Taoist tradition talks of 'the Way', which has a dynamic quality we should associate with God.

There is a thing confusedly formed,
Born before heaven and earth.
Silent and void
It stands alone and does not change,
Goes round and does not weary . . .
It is capable of being the mother of the world.
I know not its name
So I style it 'the way'.[1]

The Zen writers speak of 'It'. The Zen archer's ambition is to reach the stage when not he shoots the arrow, but 'It' shoots, and the whole Buddhist tradition supports the idea that one's own 'I' is part of a universal 'I-ness' and that one's spiritual development lies in recognising and acknowledging the fact, until we discover that we do not breath – we are breathed. 'It' flows through us all the time – if only we will let go of the illusion that it is we who are in control.

Hindu belief 'teaches that the ultimate attainment of the soul is reabsorption into Brahma, the source of all things. Maya, the veil of illusion which is the cause of the feeling of individuality, will be dissolved away and only the eternal unity of all things will remain.'[2]

In recent years we have seen psychological attempts to describe the God-experience, more particularly those of C. G. Jung. Jung quotes the alchemical saying that 'God is an infinite circle whose centre is everywhere and circumference nowhere.' Man's unconscious revolves around this centre.

1. *Tao te Ching*, Lao Tzu, tr. D. C. Lau, Penguin.
2. *Freud and Christianity*, R. S. Lee, Penguin (new ed.).

We can hardly avoid the impression that the unconscious process moves in a spiral path around a 'centre' that it slowly approaches, the 'properties' of the 'centre', meanwhile, showing themselves always more clearly. We could also put it the other way round and say that the central point, unknowable in itself, acts like a magnet upon the disparate materials and processes of the unconscious and, like a crystal grating, catches them one by one . . . It seems as if the personal complications and the dramatic, subjective climaxes that make up the quintessence of life and its whole intensity were but hesitation or timid shrinking before the finality of this strange or uncanny process of crystallisation . . . One often has the impression that the personal psyche chases around this centre like a shy animal, fascinated and frightened at the same time, always running away and yet always approaching.[3]

Jung describes man as recognising, or reflecting, God through the Self, 'that vital centre in the psyche which possesses the greatest charge of energy. Every content that is anywhere near this supercharged centre receives from it a numinous power, as though "possessed" by it.'[4]

Most religious traditions have struggled with the idea that God is part of, or is within, or is the individual human psyche. When asked who God was, William Blake replied, 'Jesus Christ. And you. And me.' 'The kingdom of God is within you,' say the Christian gospels and Eckhart states

3. *Psychology and Religion*, C. G. Jung, Vol. 14 Collected Works, Routledge and Kegan Paul.
4. *The Integration of the Personality*, C. G. Jung, Routledge and Kegan Paul.

that 'When God made man the innermost heart of the Godhead was put into man.'

> I am the image of God : therefore if
>> God would see
> Himself, He must look down, and see
>> Himself in me

as Angelus Silesius puts it. Yet Christianity in its careful delineations of a personal God who is external to the individual, even if he reflects him in some part of himself, has recognised, perhaps unconsciously, the danger which lies in the identification with God — that of megalomania. Under the effects of LSD normal people believe themselves to be God or Christ rather as schizophrenics have sometimes done, and it suggests, though no more than that, that a delusion of omnipotence, the omnipotence of the infant perhaps, is always temptingly around the corner. The emphasis on the *person* of God in Christianity — at least of a person who is all-powerful and all-wise — seems to encourage this kind of confusion in a way that a belief in 'It' is unlikely to do.

But the difficulty goes far beyond megalomania, and the ambiguity in Christianity about whether God is, or is not, inside one, touches upon a much more important problem. This is the problem of projection. The Judaeo-Christian belief that man is made in the image of God can be turned neatly on its head by the suggestion that in fact it is God who is made in the image of man. Primitive man according to some, though not all, anthropologists, projected all his fears on to external objects, rather as children often do. A mountain, or the sunrise, or a whirlpool or a dark hole, seemed to crystallise his hope or his panic until it became in itself a sacred experience (representing the process of growth within him which he felt as mysterious) or a devilish experience (representing the destructive quality of terror). It seems possible for him to have extrapolated from this to manufacture a God of even greater mysteriousness (or even greater devilishness) whom he did not need to see at all but whom his inner feelings described. The God of Judaism, who has so deeply influenced Christianity, is *too* like man – in the Old Testament we can watch his paranoia, his hunger for praise, his pique at being rejected or let down, his fits of temper and sulks – and it is impossible not to feel that some wish-fulfilment has gone on somewhere.

The awareness of the possibility of projection, an awareness heightened by the uncanny resemblance between God and man, adds to the embarrassment intelligent people now feel about God. They sense a childishness here of which they do not wish to have any part, fearing that man has manufactured a puppet-God, who can now be seen as nothing but a wrinkled glove.

Yet is it God who is the wrinkled puppet or is it the metaphor, now worn out and useless so far as twentieth-century man is concerned? The way out of this particular cul-de-sac is to reject the metaphor and to discover the metaphors which for us still have a numinous life. This is not so much a matter of looking for mystery (since although numinosity is invariably accompanied by mystery, mystery in itself signifies nothing but 'not knowing') as of looking for the areas of our life which throb with meaning, and which seem to us to be part of a process of growth. It is the *process* which has for us the same attraction, the same haunting beauty, the same terror, the same moral compulsion, which men used to attach to the idea of God. When we admit the force of the process then our lives have meaning, serious choices, and movement — a movement towards freedom and love.

As we begin to feel this process working within us, and especially as we feel ourselves moving towards greater freedom, then perhaps we can bring greater charity and insight to the traditional metaphor of God. If, at an earlier stage of the process, men found themselves turning their own experience of joy and terror into God, was this an expression of an original kind, or was it an awareness that joy and terror *are* numinous, are a reflection of the deepest truth known to man? To take another example — should we dismiss the drive towards knowledge of and union with God as an attempt to recover the unity and bliss of the womb, or must we go on from there and wonder whether the child in the womb itself expresses (reflects) a truth about the way life is? Are we imagining things when we think we discern a pattern which runs through life, through small things as well as great, and which we continually recognise under the different guises? Is it this that lies behind our metaphor of God, the pattern which Taoism calls 'the forefather of God'?

If we cannot praise, worship, enjoy, contemplate God (that is, indulge in the practices of a lover) perhaps instead we can set ourselves to pay attention to the pattern. We want to grow. If we do no more than note, and try to assist, the process of growth within us and around us, we

are engaged upon a religious exercise of the greatest pro-
fundity. It requires our attention, what the Zen archers
spoke of as a 'purposeless tension' and contemplation is
the name for this attentiveness and this tension. In the
early stages this can be undisciplined – coolness in noting
the pattern and spontaneity in submitting to it are what
matters most. Later, as the attentiveness becomes more
constant and the tension more demanding, contemplation
establishes a discipline of its own – of silence, withdrawal,
detachment from distractions. Articulateness about the
experience becomes less rather than more.

'One who knows does not speak; one who speaks does
not know.'[5]

Is this contemplation as it has been traditionally under-
stood in the West? I believe that it is. The attentiveness
of the contemplative has made him aware of the essentially
metaphorical way in which the word God is used (by himself as by others), and the deeper his experience the better
he knows that he is always talking figuratively. The most
striking thing about Western mysticism as opposed to
Eastern mysticism is the personal note that it has struck.
Western mystics described God as a father, a mother, a
brother, a lover, as well as a king and a judge. Undoubtedly
early experiences of parental and family relationships, as
well as more public relationships were projected into the
experience of God, limiting and qualifying the experience
that any particular individual actually did have.

The Christian Church has limited and qualified its
experience in a different way, insisting in its creeds (as a
bulwark against heresy) that God was three persons in one

5. *Tao te Ching.*

44

person, and those persons consisting of a father, a son, and a disembodied spirit. This was a tragic act, fixing the metaphor in a way that no metaphor should be fixed, fitting God into a comprehensible human framework that could be intensely meaningful to those to whom father-relationships or son-relationships were intensely meaningful, but was bound to be less meaningful to those to whom life-giving relationships were with women. It was also a comic act, like Canute telling the sea to go backwards – an attempt to bind what cannot be bound, and to limit or control what man has no power to limit or control. This literalism, though providing an immediate strength in the struggle against heresy, has in the long run prevented the questioning, the lively exploration into the experience of God which is needed if religion is to reach the intellectually virile.

There are, and will continue to be, people for whom the father and son aspects of God are still full of meaning, but we can no longer expect that this metaphor will work for everyone, and there seems no good reason that it should be expected to.

One of the important things about the contemplative experience is that it is not necessarily experienced in those intensely personal terms at all. For some people the sense of a close personal relationship to God is what is most meaningful, for others (by no means all in the East), the sense of moving towards, or revolving around, a centre is the most noticeable feature of their experience. For others, there is the sense of being part of the natural world, and for others yet again, perhaps the majority, *both* per-

45

sonal and impersonal encounters with the numinous form part of their experience.

When we take the contemplative experience seriously — that is to say, when we recognise that it is indispensable to our humanity and our growth — then we are liable to experience numinosity in any one of a number of ways. According to conditioning and temperament we may experience it in personal or impersonal form; potentially we can experience it in both. This is not surprising, since we are recognising that we are part of, and contributing to, a process, and that the process has a quality which is reflected in the ordinary human sense of the person. At some times we shall be more aware of the process itself, the Taoist Way, at other times more aware of the 'I-ness' of the process, the 'I-ness' profoundly expressed in Judaic and Christian belief. If we are not 'provincial' in our sympathies, but are prepared to try to achieve some sort of wholeness we shall be prepared to receive transcendent experience in both these modes. We may find ourselves perceiving ourselves as part of the natural world, caught up in the ancient process of birth, growth, maturity, decay, death and rebirth. We may become intensely aware of opposites, drawn into the conflict which surrounds suffering and healing, good and evil. We may have ecstatic experience, experiencing the sort of unity with the world which the Buddhists call 'satori', or the sort of unity which made many of the Christian saints think of God as a lover. Probably, because of our fear and our inability to 'let go' we shall know only faint glimmers of such transcendence, but they will be the glimmers which save ourselves and others from the blindness of total darkness.

The attempt made by Jung to describe the numinous experience is stated in terms of 'archetypes'. 'Archetypes' live in man's unconscious, ancestral truths which are still nuclei of power and emotion. The imagery which surrounds them has great power images of wisdom, of healing, of seduction – and these can be creative or destructive. Jung suggests that they are creative to the extent to which we become aware of their mythological influence in our lives, destructive when we let ourselves be ridden by them, preferring a kind of luxurious submission to them to the pain of detachment and self-awareness.

One of the most interesting is Christ as an archetypal image of the Self, that reflection of the God-experience in man which makes it possible for him to respond to the call towards wholeness, towards a unifying experience. Christ is the journeying hero who endures joy and pain, death and rebirth, and the agony of crucifixion is seen as the deathly experience of conflict faithfully undergone until it yields its unimaginable, and creative result. Christ is the human experience seen in section, as it were, and even if we do not begin to share conventional Christian belief, we may perhaps recognise the similarity of the Christ-experience to states of mind that we have undergone, and which we have seen others undergo.

Jung's warning about detachment from the archetype comes in useful here. We may feel the powerful pull of the archetype in our longing to heal others, to love them unselfishly, to sacrifice ourselves for them, but unless we can also see how limited are our resources, how fickle our emotions, and how great our own need, then we shall become possessed as by devils. Christ is us. We are not

Christ. This perhaps sums up the process of detaching ourselves painfully, and necessarily, from the archetype. Not to do so would be a kind of madness. Yet not to engage with the archetype would involve a stunting of the personality.

Blake's claim that God is 'Jesus Christ. And you. And me,' catches the strange, flickering experience of truth. Truth is about revelation – a religious jargon word, which is partly about the unfolding of particular patterns in time, i.e. history – but more important is about our own experience of pattern in our individual lives. With or without religion, certain patterns of experience seem to each of us to spell meaning – limited meaning if we are deeply distrustful of man and his pattern making, boundless meaning if we are too trustful, moderate meaning if we resist the temptations of credulity on the one hand and total scepticism on the other.

Revelation involves the discovery that the pattern that we know so well from our own lives interacts with other patterns both larger and smaller to a point where the word 'accident' becomes almost meaningless. Truth, we discover, works on different levels at once, has an outer and an inner side to it. Christianity has taken this sort of revelation one step further and claimed that God is the inside of our human experience, the myth of which all other myths and stories and beliefs are fragments. To be human we must love, must be vulnerable, must endure our desolate crucifixions so that new life can grow in and through us. Not to live in this way is to lose our human identity. God, in this sense, *is* 'Jesus Christ. And you. And me.'

It is within this area of human wisdom that the contemplative chooses to spend his time, giving himself up to tracing the pattern, hopeful that this will be creative for others.

Yet the texture of the contemplative experience does not really lie here. Despite moments when he sees clearly, moments of ecstasy and moments of crisis, his habitual state of mind will probably be of a very different kind. This is because transcendental experience very quickly teaches us that we cannot experience very much, or very fast, in this area. It needs patience and the tedious emptiness of waiting, the long-drawn out path of *not* experiencing. Knowing God not by his presence but by his absence (as one might appreciate a human being when missing him), is known as *via negativa*. The contemplatives of *via negativa* believe that God, as he is in himself, is unknowable, since the human senses must always break down when confronted with so great a reality. They cannot even describe at all adequately what they do experience, since the imagery is a lie the moment it is spoken, so they choose to try to know God and to live with him in a bareness of living that leaves no room for anything but the presence of God, and failing that (as the contemplative is always failing it) the emptiness when the presence is not felt. 'Look that nothing live in thy working mind but a naked intent stretching into God,' says the author of the *Epistle of Privy Counsel*, and in another book the same writer says, 'Try to penetrate that darkness above you. Strike that thick cloud of unknowing with the sharp dart of longing love, and on no account whatever think of giving up.' This state of unknowing also involves a detachment towards the created world, the detachment which, in every school of mysticism, and in every religion, has led some people into the practice of ascetic disciplines in the belief that these led to a longed-for inner freedom.

This kind of ascetism is for very few, and like many of the paths trodden by contemplatives, it requires the most careful and continued scrutiny to distinguish pathological urges from urges which represent movement towards wholeness. Most people are not aware of such a call, yet they may feel the strongest attraction to make some sense of the 'God-feeling' within them, and be overwhelmed by feelings of sickness, sadness, depression and despair if they suppress it because they disagree with conventional kinds of religious belief, or are afraid that others will think them mad or odd. If it is true that 'this is a society that represses transcendence' then they will find it painful to begin with to admit to being driven by such an improper longing, but if they can get past this stage they will discover that most people have a very good idea what they are talking about and are suppressing similar longings and experiences of their own.

I believe that learning to admit transcendence may be one of the major undertakings of a man's life, perhaps the major undertaking, so that if it is ignored his personality may be stunted or destroyed. We are all contemplatives to a greater or lesser degree, and we all need, to the limit of our capacity, to admit the experience which we may, or may not, call God.

Prayer

Prayer

It may be questioned what a word like prayer is doing in a book which is trying to sit loosely to organised religion and to talk simply about a particular human function called contemplation. The word 'prayer' is full of religious overtones which are nearly as embarrassing as God. It sounds like 'little boy kneels at the foot of the bed', and sentimental Victorian ballads, and comedians saying 'God bless you' and almost everything that gives sensitive people a *frisson* of distaste.

The trouble is that there *is*, as yet, no other word which does justice to the particular kind of attention I am trying to describe, the attention which Eastern Orthodox describe as 'holding the mind in the heart'. It isn't thinking, it isn't daydreaming, it isn't sleeping, it isn't talking, it isn't listening (at least when it works it isn't; in practice it easily slips into one or another of these things). It *is* a kind of tension, but a tension which can only come when there has been an inner relaxation, just as the Zen archer can only shoot his arrow correctly if his muscles are properly relaxed, so that they 'look on impassively'. Yet as with the archer a desperate longing to reach the target is a mistake;

the contemplative needs the same 'purposeless tension', a kind of gaiety of approach.

How do we get this 'purposeless tension'? Not, in my view, by words. Those who use words to pray (when alone, I mean – corporate prayer is rather different) are not engaged in contemplative prayer, but in something quite different. Contemplatives *may* use words, but in a particular incantatory, almost self-hypnotising way, or to give the mind something by which, temporarily, it may orientate itself. They are not talking, to God or to anyone else.

The 'purposeless tension' is achieved by mastering disciplines of relaxation, by self-awareness, by becoming aware of one's setting in the world, and finally by embarking upon an inner journey. The journey is not to 'catch' God, even though it moves in the direction of what men have called God. It is to become what is in one to become.

Sitting

The Zen word for disposing oneself to prayer is 'sitting', and the Eastern position for prayer has, of course, been to sit cross-legged in one of several postures in the belief that this reduced the circulation of blood in the legs, and increased the supply to the brain, so helping meditation. The lotus posture and its variations had a kind of easy discipline about them. The body was not tortured by an unnatural position, but maintained enough rigidity not to fall off to sleep too easily. It mirrored what was going on in the mind, the tension-in-relaxation, or relaxation-in-tension which made a particular kind of concentration possible. It was comfortable enough to be maintained for hours at a stretch, yet disposed of all choice about where to put the limbs. Even the hands were controlled by the same relaxed discipline, and allowed to lie, palms upward, upon the knees, as if receiving.

To equate the word 'sitting' with prayer is strange to us because even in prayer we tend to think in terms of achievement. We want to get somewhere with it and we therefore lose sight of it as a simple function in its own right – something men *do*, not necessarily to achieve anything but because that is the sort of creatures they are. To 'sit' is, obviously, not to move about. It also, especially if it involves getting into the lotus position, involves a temporary giving up of activity, a surrender of the active side of oneself in order to enter a mode of life which cannot be experienced in activity. It is the 'other half' of being a human being, the Mary in us who counterbalances the Martha.

In the West the traditional prayer positions have been standing and kneeling. I guess that our ancestors may have been much better at standing for long periods than we are (as late as the seventeenth century people used to stand to listen to sermons which often went on for several hours), but there is about standing the implication that one may not be able to keep it up for very long – that one is going to grow tired or be able to move quickly away. The suggestion of *timelessness*, or anyhow of permanence, which sitting conveys, is no longer there. On a more mundane level we know the added sense of security we get when someone we are trying to talk to sits down instead of standing, or wandering about the room. We know that there is a better chance of our being listened to attentively, that they are not already mentally in another place.

The other traditional Western position has been kneeling. Once again I suspect our forebears may have been more robust than we are, but except for those cast in the heroic mould it seems unlikely that men and women were able to keep up such a formidably uncomfortable position for very long. Kneeling, together with the development of it also found in the West, prostration, also has a particular implication – that of submission, humility, penitence, abasement. These emotions, though they arouse wrath among the opponents of religion, and, increasingly, embarrassment among the adherents, do not seem to me inappropriate. Man, confronted by transcendence, will inevitably experience these emotions at times – it would be pathological not to do so. But the question is whether these emotions, and the position which reflects them, represent the spectrum of transcendental experience at all adequately. Judaeo-Christian thinking had dwelt particularly hard upon this aspect of man's relationship to God to the point where it has sometimes seemed to be wilfully ignoring other, less dependent, sides to man's character – his cheerful, competent, confident, and unapologetic sides. It is as if the knob got stuck at his guilt, depression and masochism, and insisted that this was the only reality about him. That side of him is still there, and still needs expression, but I am doubtful whether further emphasis upon it is going to help him. Kneeling no longer seems an expression of the way a man feels (except at times).

West, like East, has had a stylised position for the hands in prayer – palms facing one another, finger-tips touching, the arms making a circle with the body enclosing emptiness. As in the lotus position, when the hands lie on the knees, the body maintains an unbroken contact with itself, as if each part was reminding the rest of its 'thereness'. But this position has fallen into almost complete disuse (so far as anyone can judge) except on formal occasions, i.e. the priest and his server at the altar, young children being taught to pray at school, or Sunday school, etc., and the argument against it is that unless the body is supported, as for instance, by a prie-dieu, the weight of the hands becomes tiring.

Since we have neglected the importance of the body in the whole process of contemplation, it is not surprising that we have neglected to think seriously about what we should require of it in prayer. The particular kind of attention we are going to require of our minds seems to demand that it should neither be too comfortable, nor too uncomfortable, that it needs a certain relaxed formality that removes the distraction of choice, that it implies immobility, if necessary for long periods.

Few Westerners, having grown up sitting on chairs, are going to brave the cross-legged position of the East, though for natural experimenters there seems room for exploring the benefits of this. But equally, lying in bed or on a sofa won't do, because the pull towards sleep is too strong. A likely possibility seems to be the same sort of conditions as we would need for a fairly concentrated, but sedentary work, such as writing – an upright chair. If we are respectful of traditional insights we may wish to go beyond this and choose a fixed position for the feet and legs, and a position for the hands which keeps them still, and in contact with the rest of the body.

Silence

The essence of contemplation is the entry into silence (or darkness), a journey which, for the most part, must be made alone. Even those contemplatives who believe in the use of some form of words, for example the Eastern *mantra* (repetition of the same word or phrase) or the Orthodox Jesus-prayer,

'Lord Jesus Christ, Son of God, have mercy upon us'
are not precisely interested in the words as any form of self-expression but as a way of moving into a deeper stillness. They are not for everyone – for some they feed into obsessive patterns which would make any real 'letting-go' impossible.

For other contemplatives, a word, a phrase, the verse of a poem or a line of song will emerge naturally out of their silence, and often tell them a great deal about their unconscious state of mind. This is a common human experience in any case, a throwing up of what the unconscious mind is trying to ignore, so that we find ourselves humming 'Oh, for the wings of a dove' on the way to an examination or the dentist, but it will occur more often and sometimes more creatively within the reflective calm of contemplation.

But when one has said that, one must go on to say that the contemplative experience is not about words at all, that it is the attempt to go beyond and behind them. It can be a maddening, frustrating, bewildering effort in which there seems nothing to hold on to, since we are trying also to go beyond what our senses can teach us about the world (the philosophical absurdity of this makes it appear no less worthwhile an attempt).

Of course, to begin with, silence is not silence at all; it is filled with our own perpetual inner chatter. As this gradually dies away we begin to feel we know the silence intimately, almost as a person. We may experience it as threatening, hostile, even as killing. We may experience it as boredom, tension, loneliness, insignificance, a state of being unloved, and as loss of identity. This dark face of silence is painful to look upon, and we long to be let off the encounter. We endure the illusion of people suffering — that their suffering is different, peculiar to them, and worse than other people's. We use every trick, every device open to us to dodge the moment we dread, the moment of 'letting go', of yielding, of opening ourselves to the torrents of inner pain. Yet it is precisely this which silence must achieve.

From this point on (which may be reached a number of times in the course of a life-time) we see the other face of silence, a face full of warmth, hope, meaning, love. Tension, boredom and loneliness disappear. There is a renewed sense of rhythm and relaxation, of order and of identity, all emerging from a state of stillness. The whole process is aptly described in the Lao Tzu.

> I do my utmost to attain emptiness;
> I hold firmly to stillness.
> The myriad creatures all rise together
> And I watch their return.
> The teeming creatures
> All return to their separate roots.
> Returning to one's roots is known as stillness.[1]

1. *Tao te Ching.*

Relaxation

The difficulty for most secular contemplatives is that they are forced to lead a life lacking in natural rhythm. They cannot get up at sunrise and go to bed at sunset, even if they wished to do so, and we have organised our social lives in such a way that it is rarely possible to follow the natural inclinations of the body for rest and inactivity after periods of fierce activity.

In a place ordered for contemplation, like a Hindu *ashram* or a Western monastery, the rhythm of life is designed to help contemplation, and exercise, diet and much else leads the body into the sort of relaxation which frees the mind for a different sort of awareness.

Those who lead an ordinary life have a more difficult job. They have frequently to contend with physical exhaustion and with social demands which encourage them to over-eat and over-drink, and to become too tired. They have too little opportunity to 'sit', to read and think, and it is often only as a result of ill-health, or during a brief annual holiday that they get the chance to strike up more than a surface acquaintance with themselves.

This seems to demand quicker, and more sophisticated techniques of relaxation than we have been accustomed to use in the West (though if we developed, as a society, a more balanced attitude to activity then we might organise our work and leisure on more 'livable' lines), and it is worth making a careful examination of ways of relaxing which may have struck us as cranky or improper in the past.

Yoga

Yoga works partly by teaching techniques for the control of muscles which makes relaxation possible, partly by poses which bring pressure upon glands and nerve centres. Some of the more important poses involve inverted postures which relieve the body of the pull of gravity in the usual direction. The most important exercises of all involve breathing control.

Brought up with an empire-building superiority to all kinds of native wisdom we have tended to mix arrogant amusement about such techniques with childish credulity about what fakirs could achieve. But as our respect for Eastern wisdom gradually increases perhaps we can be realistic and unprejudiced enough to look seriously at systems of exercise such as this and discover by experiment what they have to offer us. It needs caution. There is a streak in all of us which longs to find magic and use it to control and impress others, and the middle-aged in particular seem susceptible to magic – in the form of religion, diet, exercise, or art – and need a lot of decorum not to get carried away by their enthusiasms. Yoga isn't magic. It is either an intelligent discipline which promotes the well-being of the body and thus of the mind or it is nothing. It seems worth trying.

Ordinary physical exercise – games, walking, swimming – are important to our ability to relax, and so to discourage over-activity. More sophisticated techniques of relaxation – sauna baths, Turkish baths, massage, may be worth the cost if they can quickly achieve the state of physical well-being that makes it possible to live at ease with one's body.

What seems to be needed is an attitude of *respect* for the body in the part that it plays in contemplative activity. The old-fashioned contempt and amusement of the intellectual at the idea of exercise will not do in this context. Contemplation forbids that kind of splitting of mind and body – the body must be treated with as much seriousness (or gaiety) as the mind. Still less will any Manichean contempt for the flesh be appropriate; in fact, a bias of that kind demands a particular emphasis on bodily awareness before any further progress is likely to be possible.

Such disciplines are not easy for us. There is tedium in them, as in any kind of regular practice, and a certain amount of embarrassment for which we may overcompensate with excessive and slightly fanatical enthusiasm. We need to tread a soberer path than this, developing an openness to experience which begins by admitting how out of touch we are with our bodies and their potentialities, and an experimental objectivity which avoids credulity.

What Happens Next

We have achieved a reasonably relaxed state of mind and body (nothing remarkable, simply the stage when we have unclenched our hands and are not obsessively worried about anything), we are prepared to sit in a position of more or less formality for a reasonable length of time (say half an hour), and we are prepared, at least consciously, to try to live in the inner space for a bit. I want to try to describe some of the things which can happen as a result.

The first time or two we try it it can be a marvellous experience. We can feel bathed in peace, a peace which laps around our minds and bodies until our breathing becomes slow and quiet. Hours later we can feel healed and unified by the experience as a writer or painter feels unified after he has finished work.

But as with writing or painting the initial bliss gives way to something costly and difficult. The writer knows that the moment will come when he is desperately, torturingly bored with what he has to do, that he will feel sleepy, depressed, headachey, ill, hungry and thirsty when the work is not going well. All these ills make themselves felt in contemplative prayer. The boredom can be the most utter misery, and the longing to sleep is often irresistible.

Why go on if this happens? Because, as a writer can tell us, this is perhaps the most crucial moment of the whole effort. Extreme boredom, he comes to discover, is a smoke-screen for fear. There are a number of kinds of fear involved in any creative activity—fear that one will not realise the inner vision, fear of self-exposure, fear of sterility—but in general the fear of the creative artist adds up to one overriding fear, the fear of giving himself. He also wants very badly to give himself—he knows that his work will be lifeless if he doesn't succeed—but the extremes of boredom, tiredness, etc., seem to coincide with the times when this inner conflict is most intense. Somewhere around this point he surrenders, he 'gives himself up', and from that moment the boredom disappears and the work flowers, though the crisis will recur constantly throughout his writing. This kind of experience is not peculiar to artists. In milder degrees we all share it whenever we try to make things, to work with our hands, to produce something good and satisfying which will affect the quality of life around us. The rhythm between tension and relaxation is inescapable for us all.

To this extent we are all contemplatives whether we know it or not, and artists explicitly recognise in themselves a form of contemplative activity – a reflection upon the experience of living, that is prepared to open itself up to unconscious depths.

In contemplative prayer, as against these other forms of contemplation, there will be less fear of failure – there is no objective standard to measure ourselves by as in the case of the book or the painting which the artist creates – but there is the same very acute fear of giving ourselves, perhaps in a stronger form, and this is heightened by the absence of distraction. The satisfying processes of applying paint, or whatever may be the technique of the creative artist, is denied, and all that may be left is the occasional use of words, crevices for the mind to cling to as it makes its lonely descent.

Why attempt something so painful? I think the honest answer must be 'Because we cannot help ourselves, because we are addicts of prayer, which is a way of saying that we find, or hope to find, something here which we cannot find elsewhere.' We have to learn to stop thinking of prayer as a duty, as organised religion has insisted for so long – one might as well say that it is a duty of the birds to sing – and recognise that we are praying animals.

Not all the time perhaps. In states of overwork, illness,

depression, at periods of strenuous creative activity, at times when we are engaged in costly personal conflicts with those we live or work with, the lack of stillness may make contemplative prayer a faint hope. But then artists often give up the direct practice of their art during war or when having, and caring for, a baby, though their experiences are treasured and eventually fed back again into their art. It is both the long-term persistence of the attempt, and the depth to which we are prepared to pursue it, which is ultimately important.

If we can manage to survive the various hazards I have described then contemplative prayer becomes something habitual – something we take for granted as part of our way of life, irrespective of whether on any particular day we happen to feel specially 'in the mood'. Waiting to feel 'in the mood' is as unsatisfactory as in most human activities; we never really know until we have begun something whether we are 'in the mood' since we are so often in the grip of doubts and fears that can only be dispelled by actually doing whatever we are doubtful about. The sense of habit gives a certain confidence which may make it possible to take liberties with our working method, as an experienced craftsman feels confident enough of his own mastery and his own capacity for self-criticism to use unorthodox methods which would be disastrous for a beginner.

But the capacity for self-criticism, together with the willingness to expose ourselves to the opinions and criticisms of others, is important, as in all things undertaken in isolation. If we do not match our inner dialogue with a dialogue with the world around us, then we can all too easily become cranky, fanatical and convinced that we are somehow 'special'. Then we are moving away from the contemplative position which is essentially one of a deepening appreciation of the 'ordinariness' of life (in all its mystery), an ordinariness which must include the ordinariness of ourselves. Unless we find ourselves becoming more 'ordinary' rather than less then we are going wrong.

Intercession

To pray for other people is an immediately attractive idea to those who are sympathetic towards others' suffering, and aware of their own helplessness in the face of it. At least it is something one can *do*, in situations (someone dying of cancer, for instance) where other forms of loving care may be of little use.

As with other forms of prayer, however, the difficulties can be formidable, and the more formidable since we are dealing with something apparently so simple.

Some of the difficulties disappear, however, if we cease to comfort ourselves with the illusion of 'doing' (arguably the best anaesthetic available to us) and accept the harder knowledge that intercession is about 'being', our own being, and that of the person prayed for. Intercessory prayer is not, in my view, about miracles, apart from the miraculous process of love itself. It isn't about trying to change physical laws so that a tumour will shrivel and disappear. It isn't about trying to patch up a marriage so that the couple will be nice to each other and all the hate will be swept under the carpet. It isn't even about praying that a rich old gentleman will appear with a cheque book just at the moment when only money can save a good cause.

If prayer is to be true it cannot be manipulative in these sorts of ways. It isn't about pushing God into something he doesn't want to do. It isn't trying to work against the physical world and its laws, even when these laws operate terribly against man. It isn't attempting to be a short cut which dodges the psychological complexities of human beings. It isn't even attempting to interfere with the humdrum legal and monetary processes of our society, destructive as these can be for individuals in certain situations. Occasionally, it must be said, prayer *does* seem, dramatically, to achieve one or another of these effects. Diseases are mysteriously halted or cured, individuals do appear inexplicably changed, offers of help are made with a timing so perfect that it seems to defy coincidence.

But this is the caviare of prayer and what it is mostly concerned with is bread and butter – the bread and butter of ordinary human beings praying for other ordinary human beings. What the saints achieve, in taking certain sorts of suffering into themselves, is not necessarily a model for others.

For what those of us who are neither holy nor humble are continually faced with is the danger of taking an inflated view of ourselves. It is a short step from praying for other people in their troubles to feeling that one has some sort of control over their troubles, and a short step from controlling their troubles to having some control, however benevolent, over them. Or we may have a different temptation to somehow claim them as *ours* – our protégés, our lame dogs, our cures. No sort of intercession which does not leave the other person in a state of total freedom is any good, and if we cannot manage to find a workable method it may be better to give up the attempt, at least temporarily, until we can.

How then can we pray for other people in a way that seeks to manipulate neither God, the world, nor the individual? We can probably only do so if we believe, or anyhow hope, that there is a harmony, or unity, in the world that is to be trusted even when appearances seem to deny it. As a Jewish prisoner wrote on a wall in Cologne:

> I believe in the sun even when it is not shining.
> I believe in love even when I cannot feel it.
> I believe in God, even when he is silent.

If there is such harmony, a harmony into which even the agonies of disease, of human conflict, of poverty and hardship play notes which make up a whole of a beauty and healing power beyond our ordinary imagination, then what is needed for ourselves and others is some kind of perception of truth.

We do not need to perceive truth very clearly ourselves to offer it to others. It is rather like being a parent who holds up a small child above the heads of the crowd so that he may see the queen go by. The father probably cannot see at all well himself, indeed he may not see at all. Nevertheless he can give the child its chance for a glimpse of glory. Intercession can be compared to holding a person so that they may be exposed to the love and beauty of God.

It is this which makes it quite different from the more usual process of offering sympathy to other people. The

offering of sympathy depends upon an act of imagination
– by putting ourselves in another person's shoes we can
enter a little into their suffering and so respond meaning-
fully to it. Intercessory prayer does not depend upon an
imaginative act – it can even be a help not to know the
details of the person prayed for. It has not the warmth,
nor the essentially emotional nature, of an ordinary sympathetic exchange, nor is the fact that it is we who are
praying important, as it would be important if it was we
who were offering sympathy. For a moment our personality, identity, our imagination, and even our own need for
love are set on one side – our only concern is that the other
should be reached by the love that is at the heart of the
human experience, or if you will, the love of God.

How do we know who to pray for? A nun who spends
much of her day in intercessory prayer described to me
how, out of the long list of people in various kinds of extreme trouble for whom she was asked to pray, one or two
would 'spring out' at her, and she would know that they
were the ones who specially needed attention in prayer.
When the mind is in a certain state of quietness and attention it can become aware in this sort of way, as it can also
become aware of the necessity for certain sorts of action,
the purpose of which it may not understand at the time –
for example, going to see someone for no obvious reason.
It is of the essence of the contemplative experience that we
should respect the unconscious processes and try to cultivate the sort of detachment which will leave us free enough
to notice them. Contemplation is about 'being in the right
place at the right time' either in the physical sense of turning up at the moment which we seem to fit, or in the sense

of being 'there' to offer intercessory prayer at the time when this is most needed.

It matters that we should be 'there' at the moment when someone needs prayer, as it matters that the father should be there to hold up the child in the crowd. Otherwise it may not see at all.

Fasting

Nowadays religious people are embarrassed by the thought of fasting, and indeed the whole battery of ascetic practices which once seemed inseparable from religious practice. The only modern experience of fasting is undertaken to improve the appearance of the body, and not with any spiritual objective. Our perception that the practice of fasting has been bound up with a contempt for the flesh (a contempt found to a greater or lesser degree in all the great world religions) has led us to reject the whole idea from the fear that it may be the symptom of a pathological state (as of course it can be).

I think it is a pity that we are cut off in this way from what was once a universal tradition because I believe that there were special insights connected to fasting (and to a lesser extent with other ascetic practices) which had a value that we have now overlooked.

On the simplest level fasting establishes a particular kind of rapport between mind and body which otherwise is easily lost. Hunger, like mild physical pain, can put us back into our body, puncturing the habitual inflation of the mind with its reminders of need. The peculiar anxiety attached to hunger (even when we know that it will not go on indefinitely) seems to root us in our humanity, a humanity which stretches back to, and has been formed by, the precariousness of nature.

Also, as with relaxation, it helps us towards discoveries about our body and our own dangerous remoteness from it. While the body has its every whim catered for we know nothing of the 'other side' of human experience, like the dark side of the moon, of what our body is like, or is, when its needs are denied. I believe that in order to be fully human we need to know both about satisfaction and denial.

Fasting is, of course, an anology for a deeper and more traumatic experience. On a day-to-day level we all, sooner or later, have to go without profound satisfactions which feel as necessary and as life-giving as food feels to us when we are hungry; on the deepest level of all our longing for God may remain painfully unsatisfied. This *via negativa* runs through all human experience and is perhaps the hardest of all human conditions to bear. It means that, whether we like it or not, there are times when we can only know about the things which make for our sense of wholeness and well-being through the pain of their absence. We know them then with a particular intensity which may transform and illuminate our subsequent having. The pleasure of eating is heightened by the hunger which precedes it.

The problem with ascetic practices is whether it is really necessary to seek them, since for most people the daily struggle supplies enough deprivation to remind them of what it is to be a human being. The conscious adoption of ascetic practices may be for those who need to think more clearly about the role that suffering plays in their lives — on the one hand the destructive effect of their own half-conscious masochism, and on the other hand the creative possibilities of trying to face the suffering which is inevitable.

Prayer in Church

There are still enough active churches in this country for people to regard the Church as a focus of interest in spiritual matters. Interest has, of course, spread far beyond the churches in recent years, and in the drug and hippie cults in particular, and in the interest in Eastern religions, we have seen how people long not just to hear God talked about, but to have some experience in depth which will bring them in touch with spiritual realities.

But what of what still goes on within the churches in this country – the baptisms and weddings, the meetings for Sunday prayer, the Communions and Masses, and the friendship and fellowship which exists alongside these occasions of corporate prayer? What is any of it trying to do? And what *does* it do?

It must be said that it is middle-class prayer that we are talking about. Church-going in working-class areas has steadily declined, even among the Roman Catholics who have been most successful in maintaining working-class congregations. But in the prosperous suburbs, in the churches in central London which can manage to provide the right atmosphere to attract the intelligentsia, and even to some extent in village churches, the mood is strongly middle-class.

Perhaps in the suburbs churchgoing has acquired a little of the American ethos. The Church seems to fit into the pattern of a 'nice' home (conflict within the family carefully concealed since it is even less acceptable than dirt in the spotless kitchen), a good job, a big car, and children at the grammar school or the private school.

Some contemporary Christians – among them Dr. Frank Lake – have suggested that what churchgoers have in common is not so much a class background, as a particular psychological background. They tend, so Dr. Lake thinks, to be depressive people, battling with perfectionism and guilt. Churchgoing appeases some of their guilt. Few parish priests would deny that there is a strong streak of neuroticism in their congregations, though considering how prevalent neurotic traits are throughout the community there is no very convincing evidence that their incidence is higher among churchgoers.

However, most of us who are involved in organised religion (I am a practising Anglican myself) are well aware that religion at its worst can offer various brands of opium. Apart from the old charge (more dubious nowadays) of churchgoing offering a certain status of respectability, there are other ways in which it can lead to unreality. Some of the dangers are sufficiently well-known – the fact that authority can feed the infantile side of people and so delay or prevent their maturity; or the way a firm moral line can prevent people asking the questions about their sexual fears and repressions which might lead towards self-knowledge; or the way that any tight little group can become a closed circle, and the closed circle in turn can become a fortress against the world; or the way that a misunderstanding of the nature of goodness can lead to self-righteousness.

There are also, I believe, less well-known dangers about

such communities, in the main those associated with the feeling of the members that they have a great deal to give in terms of practical help to others, or that they have a precious contribution in seminal ideas. This smugness too easily masks inner poverty – it is painful for individuals or a community to admit their emptiness and lostness (which admission alone can lead back into creativity).

None of these dangers are peculiar to the churches. If they are more clearly seen there than in other kinds of organisation it is because, despite all their faults and failings, the churches are still braver about attempting community than almost anyone else. They fail because they try, which is a very different and much nobler failure than the failure which results from inertia.

If it be asked what any of this has to do with contemplation and with prayer I would say a great deal. Contemplation can only result from a sense that one has coped courageously with one's environment and with one's inner problems; it is not an escape from successful activity but a development from it. It is this which gives prayer meaning and integrity.

As we come to look at the forms of prayer which go on inside churches, and privately among the individuals who go to church, I want to make the assertion that it is only in the degree to which any congregation has achieved some genuine sense of community, and only in the degree to which the individuals who make it up have really struggled with their problems, that the services are more than a gentle anaesthetic. This is perhaps easy to see if we take the example of marriage. If the couple who are getting married have reached the point of seeing love as a really courageous attempt at self-giving; if their respective parents, who will probably be in the congregation, have given them over the years some kind of example of integrity (however stormy) rather than neurotic evasion; if the priest who marries them, whether married or not, has coped well with his own sexuality; finally, if some of the married people in the congregation have really tried to live their marriages, then the couple will say the words of the marriage vows, and the listening congregation will hear them, with a particular resonance which would be impossible if the marriage was undertaken frivolously or neurotically, or was frivolously or neurotically witnessed.

Marriage is so near to the nub both of human joy and of human suffering that it is not difficult for a wedding service to be meaningful for those who take part. But the more general joys and pains of human existence are the ingredients of which other Church services are composed, and when these are lifeless, stereotyped and dull it is because life has somehow got left outside the Church. It is not a matter of whether a Church uses ritual, like the Roman Catholic Church, or refuses it, like the Society of Friends. The fairly rigid forms of ritual can flower with meaning as easily as the looser forms which depend upon spontaneity. In this garden there is room for many different kinds of plant. It is only a matter of whether some human growth is taking place in that community and/or in the individuals, since there can be no poetry, no grace, no beauty, no spirituality, without it.

What should the individual expect to give or to take from a Church service? Sooner or later he must ask of it that it gives him an experience which he cannot have at home on his own (or is less likely to have), an experience (in religious language) of transcendence, in Jungian language an 'archetypal experience', in his own words some sense of things 'falling into place'. Without this sense of meaning, he is the victim of an empty habit, and the habit itself can probably become an obstacle to any satisfying 'experiencing' since it denies him the chance to look at anything that happens within the walls of a church with fresh, surprised eyes.

I say 'sooner or later' because experiencing in this way is by no means as likely as it is with certain drugs. As with all repeated human activities there is inevitable boredom, which in turn can give way to an aridity of the spirit which it is painful and frustrating to bear. Boredom is as inescapable in churchgoing as it is, at times, in marriage, and as with marriage, there can be different reasons for it. The reasons can lie in the external circumstances; the Church service can be clumsy, stupid, childish, unimaginative, self-absorbed, as can an unsatisfactory mate: but equally, the reasons can lie within us; we can be bored because we are afraid of the depths to which relationship is taking us, or because we do not want to give ourselves.

Although there are situations of boredom in which the remedy is to seek stimulation, in general we learn that it pays us in life to contain our boredom, since certain developments within us – of learning, loving, self-knowledge, trust – can only take place if we endure the suffering of boredom.

It is not surprising if we seek refuge from the drama enacted in our churches in boredom, since the drama may make huge demands upon us. For instance, in the case of the Mass, or Holy Communion, it requires us, in the middle of our humdrum concerns with work and family, cooking and sleep, to look at human life in section. In the life and death of Christ, we are invited to trace out the inmost agony and joy of our humanity; in whatever the dress in which it is disguised in our own lives we can recognise, when we can bear to, a pattern of love, crucifixion and resurrection with which we are perfectly familiar. It is not surprising if, every Sunday, we cannot open ourselves to something so profoundly meaningful – we could not open ourselves, with such regularity, to the world's most sublime drama, say to *Hamlet* or *Oedipus Rex*. But regularity acts, perhaps quite properly, as a tranquilliser for what is beyond us to comprehend too often. Sometimes the veils are withdrawn (I think there are few regular churchgoers who do not know this experience), and we are touched by the glory which accompanies a sudden unity of vision. A certain resignation to regularity, as a resignation to the duller periods of marriage, can make us less aggressively and painfully demanding of 'experience', quietly hopeful that our turn will come when we are ready for it, and eventually we are reasonably satisfied. It is necessary to notice, over a period of time, that our frustration stems as much from inner problems and difficulties as from the imaginative poverty of Church religion. Inner and outer poverty are inextricably related.

If what we hope to get from a Church service is some poetic and imaginative life, together with a security which can let us swim fairly serenely through deep waters, what can we give back? Perhaps more vocal demandingness about the ways in which we feel disappointed and deprived, together with a good deal more thought about what works and what doesn't and why. The man in the pew easily turns into a pudding, moulded by clergymen into a dull obedience. Resentments build up to the point where he insists on his puddingness as a kind of revenge for years of boredom; he won't countenance even minute changes in the form of service, he is scandalised by any change in the building or the ornaments, he is prepared to block any new idea. He has been moulded so effectively into an imitation of lifelessness that he has forgotten how to live.

This takes us on to consider what the Church community should be giving to and taking from its liturgical life. Its difficulty is to maintain the balance between continuity and experiment. Continuity is essential if those who come to pray are going to be given the peace in which to move into stillness, yet if there is no experiment, or, more disturbingly, no wish for experiment, then it is a sign that sterility has crept into the Church's life. Where people are experiencing, and not just anaesthetising themselves against the painful lack of movement and joy in their lives, then some creative expression of this becomes almost unavoidable. It becomes important that the outer world (in this case, the Church service) should be influenced, illuminated, invigorated, by the inner vision, and then the old drabness and timidity becomes unendurable.

Parish churches, it seems to me, might consider a kind of 'workshop' approach to corporate prayer, perhaps allowing themselves one experimental service a month or at festivals in which the words, movement, and music were of people's own choice or making, the most accurate expression possible of their real needs or feelings. This could probably only be done with integrity by a group of people who had all got to know one another extremely well, well enough to say what they really thought at least some of the time, and in a modern town parish this would probably mean the group going away together for a weekend and so losing some of the inhibitions which hinder lively discussion. It would certainly involve a wide range of talents, since effective liturgy may require an ability to dance, sing, act, play musical instruments, or an ability to write, design and make clothes, or, a profound knowledge of the symbolism, psychological and theological, which surrounds man's need to worship. I think myself that it all also involves some genuine and determined attempt at corporate silence, together with some subsequent and continuing discussion about what effect the silence has of either a positive or negative kind. For instance, do we become aware of disturbing elements in our corporate life – feelings of aggression, hatred, fear? Or can we move, by it and through it, into some new awareness of our neighbour and our relation to him that we had not known before? In our ignorance of silence (the Quakers being the sterling exception to this) we have little idea of what we may expect to find if we open ourselves courageously to being with other people without the defensive chatter of the cocktail party to protect us.

In these ways (which are not for everyone) I believe that many more might be led into an experience of the numinous. Not, of course, that the life of the religious man, in or out of the Church, should be a pursuit of numinous experience. Numinous experience, like the perfect orgasm (not as crude a comparison as it sounds, since both are an experience, totally convincing, of life in unity), becomes more elusive the harder we seek it. This is not surprising since both experiences, to succeed, demand a 'letting go' of the self, and an aggressive 'seeking' makes this difficult, if not impossible. Nevertheless, while neither a Church nor an individual, if wise, allows the search for the numinous to become compulsive, both may hope to cultivate the quality of life in such a way that the numinous may at times be found there. This healing, centring experience of wholeness liberates from the despair, the meaninglessness, the addictive illnesses, the materialism and the sterility which all too easily devour us.

Ecstasy

One of the incidentals of contemplative experience is ecstatic experience – moments when the world suddenly appears in a quite different guise from usual, being suffused by light, colour, beauty and meaning. The ecstatic subject suddenly sees himself in a quite different light in relation to the world around him – he may become aware that he is inextricably a part of the natural world – or he may have an overwhelming impression of a loving personal God. Such moments have such a profound conviction of reality that those who experience them remember them for a life-time. They feel that, for a little while, a veil has been removed and shown them a glimpse of something for which they long. But even if it is unattainable, the belief that it exists is a wonderful reassurance.

Nevertheless, it *is* an incidental experience, and one to which people at certain ages, and in certain states of mind seem exceptionally prone. To attempt to manoeuvre the mind into the experience, to 'conjure' God, feels a dishonourable action, at least to those who have already embarked on some sort of contemplative journey (at the beginning it may be different). I expect, however, it is possible to be too puritanical about this. The Christian Church, although it has not practised the taking of drugs as a way in to ecstatic experience, has used methods such as fasting and sleeplessness, which almost certainly made such supra-normal states more likely. Aldous Huxley suggests that prolonged fasting set up certain chemical changes in the body which were conducive to hallucinatory states, and going without sleep is known to have a hallucinogenic effect.

Nor should we forget the part that group practices have played in the Church in leading people into visionary experience – dancing to the point of frenzy, 'shaking', speaking with tongues, public confession of sins, eloquent preaching, music of the negro spiritual type, have all achieved this sort of result at one time or another. It seems likely that there has been a strong unconscious wish for the unifying effect of ecstatic experience, and that this has again and again produced a successful method.

We can no longer do it unconsciously as our ancestors did, and since we are learning more and more about the physiological conditions which produce such states, and how to achieve them, we are approaching the point where we may have a real choice whether or not to submit ourselves to ecstatic states.

In talking about ecstasy I must mention the more 'ordinary' sense in which many people have experienced ecstasy – in the course of sexual experience. At first sight this may appear removed from religious experience, yet the crucial ingredient – that of the sense of unity – is present in both types of ecstasy, and it is this sense of unity which, for man, marks 'religious' experience and leads into the hunger for God. Sex, like the Japanese 'satori', like the Western 'conversion' experience, like certain kinds of group experience in which the divisions of fear between individuals break down so that they become 'sent', is capable of giving man something for which he desperately longs (in a psychic as well as a physical sense), though it can also be as elusive as the others in yielding precisely the result longed for. But the deep sensuality which is so obvious in mystical writing, and of which extreme asceticism is perhaps merely an oblique expression, suggests that sexuality is inseparable from deep spirituality. My own belief is that neither sexuality nor spirituality are capable of their fullest development if due weight is not given to the part which both play in the personality. They are a kind of Siamese twins, neither of which can live apart from the other's well-being.

The possibility of obtaining ecstatic experience from drugs has produced fastidious horror among many religious people, and this strikes me as a proper distaste once a strongly based belief has been established, or as long as the belief continues to nourish and stretch the personality. But it is easy to ignore the kind of agony of searching for meaning which one often finds among the late adolescent and again, sometimes, in middle-age, an agony which may need relief or at any rate, informed opinion, at least as badly as any of the agonies of the body. What may be needed is, on the religious level, an experience as total, as single-minded, as falling in love is on the personal level, and it may be quite as necessary in leading us into new ways of living and new adventures of relationship. The Church, if it is to have life henceforward, must think deeply and seriously about the human need for such authentic 'single-minded' experiences, since it is in the memory of, or the hope of, such experiences that men struggle and strive. Hitherto they have been present, in some form, throughout Christian history, as well as in the history of all other religions. They begin to die out, as a religion begins to die, and it is as religion dies, that men begin to demand the unifying experience in ways that defy man's traditional experience and which scorn his traditional wisdom.

Life

The principle of non-activity, of 'waiting', comes so strangely to us in the West that often we can make no sense of it, and in our fear we are quick to dub it 'anti-life'. By conducting our discussions of the subject in a particular loaded way, e.g. should we feed the starving? we manage to convince ourselves that passivity is not only useless, but wicked, virtue being then defined in terms of works which can be immediately shown to produce some beneficial result. The special forms of suffering which we associate with some Eastern countries – for example, the corruption, starvation and disease of a city like Calcutta – are adduced by us to spring from the contemplative stance of Eastern religion with its disinterest in reform.

It may well be true that our own activist temperament, including the activist temperament of Western Christianity, has contributed very largely to a state of affairs in many Western countries in which virtually no one dies in the street, or of starvation. The soaring industrial prosperity which eventually (though slowly) lifted even the lowest-paid workers up to and above the bread line was clearly associated with a very positive belief in the virtue of work, a virtue which has commended itself to Protestantism more than to Catholicism.

To lift people from a condition of desperate want is no mean feat and it would be folly not to value this, not to value it as perhaps the supreme achievement of the West. Nevertheless we must go on from this point to ask whether most people do feel themselves rich in the more profound meanings of the word, and we are forced to recognise that, freed from the desperate preoccupation with hunger and employment, men and women have discovered new areas of indigence in their lives. The rapid increases in neurotic forms of illness, the rise in the suicide figures, the growing problem of addiction to drugs or alcohol, the random evidence of widespread sexual unhappiness, does not suggest that we live in a society in which there is very much joy and contentment. Nobody has learned more thoroughly than we have that man does not live by bread alone.

What does he live by then? Not by absence of bread, nor contempt for the faithful toil which produces it. It is too easy to turn a cherished belief on its head and insist that its opposite is true. But problems of great complexity are not solved in this way but by an unusual openness to contradictory elements in a situation, and a flexibility in dealing with them. Man's active side is one of the most precious gifts he has and the only way in which he could possibly have survived in a world that has often been cold and harsh; it is the side by which he controls his environment.

But it represents only half of him. If activity represents the side of man which controls his environment, then passivity, or what I have called 'contemplation', represents the side of him which recognises that he is part of his environment, and at one with it. He is formed of the same matter as the life which surrounds him, and from the moment of conception the same current of life has flowed through him as flows through all else. He is deeply at one with all creation and at times can know this with the purest joy. This is his 'ancestry', his 'background', the source from which he comes and to which he must return. Man can only be happy, I suggest, if at fairly regular intervals in his life he renews his awareness of this ground in which he is rooted. 'Returning to one's roots is known as stillness,' says Lao Tzu, and the alternative to such stillness may well be the frenetic busyness that does not know how to stop, or to sit still, or even to sleep. Robbed of his stillness man is driven to stimulants to keep him at work when his exhausted body can no longer continue, and tranquillisers to enforce the rest and relaxation which he has lost the trick of achieving for himself.

What I believe we need in this situation is not a sudden Easternising of ourselves, a wholesale selling out to gurus and fakirs, or even to contemplative prayer. The immediate need seems to be for something much more modest and down-to-earth, a simple recognition that we are *rhythmical* creatures, creatures who, obviously enough, need to follow bursts of strenuous activity with periods of rest and quietness; creatures who, less obviously (and this is where we touch upon deep fears), will have a natural tendency to follow periods of rest and quietness with periods of strenuous activity. The second is much more difficult to believe. When we made work into a virtue we made laziness into a sin, and as with all sins, we have a secret conviction that everyone (including ourselves) is dying to commit them. Ignoring our deep-felt *need* to work, and the rhythm which we can see at work in nature wherever we look, we think and talk continually as if laziness were our temptation. But is it? Is it still? Or is work, and the perfectionism which accompanies it, now the greater temptation?

If we are continually lashing ourselves to work at times when we do not feel like it, then we lose contact with, and confidence in, the natural voices within us which tell us to rest when we are tired, or to be active when we are energetic. If we overrule these voices often enough and for long enough, either by the strength of our will, or by the use of artificial aids such as drugs, then we forget how to listen even as they become more and more insistent, until often the first time that we hear them is when we are struck down by a disabling illness.

But it does not seem impossible that, just as we are learning a new respect for nature because of the desperate threat of pollution, so we may learn a new respect for the workings of our own exhausted and mismanaged bodies. We may learn to think again about the signals our over-civilised bodies put out – skin complaints, indigestion, constipation, allergies, insomnia – not in any hypochondriacal way but as signals of lives that have gone wrong. Perhaps we may come to see that if the word 'sin' still has meaning then these simple, everyday problems from which none of us is exempt, may help in sounding out the 'wrongness' of our lives.

I began by talking about rhythm, the rhythm between

busyness and rest, between activity and passivity, because I think it is a sense of this rhythm that we most badly need, and it is almost impossible to talk about rhythm without going on to speak of self-awareness.

To live within a sense of rhythm means that, on a simple level at least, we must stay in touch with our own physical needs, knowing, as a cat knows, the time to rest and the time to refrain from resting. Like the Zen archer we learn how to wait for 'It', the compelling purpose which signals the moment for action. Obviously our own tiredness or energy is not the only way in which we can know the working of 'It'. A hungry, crying baby, someone in need or distress or danger, a customer waiting to be served, a meal to be cooked, has an 'Itness' of its own that we cannot neglect. Yet there is a difference between performing such duties when we are in touch with our bodies from within, not driving them like unwilling slaves. If we can carry out even the most routine tasks recognising that we and those for whom we perform them are alike caught up in the 'Itness' of things, then a new gracefulness, a new sense of relaxation, enters our work. It is as if action and contemplation have run together, making possible the healing kind of 'thereness' for which we have longed all our lives, and of which we have only caught tantalising glimpses, usually from watching the movements of more primitive peoples.

Since we are not primitive people, however, then our awareness can extend from physical self-awareness to psychological awareness. We learn to know something about experience not just from within, e.g. the feeling in the arm when we would like to slap someone, the feeling we associate with hunger, thirst, sexual desire, sleep, or the urge to sneeze, but also from without. We can learn how to observe ourselves and others in such a way as to make intelligent deductions which go far beyond a simple awareness of our needs. This kind of deduction has taken man a very long way from his simple beginnings, making it possible for him to wield complex forms of power in technological, economic, political and psychological fields. Armed with this knowledge and the power that it gives, man becomes much more formidable, since his mistakes can occur on a much larger scale than before, and can be destructive of life – human, animal, or vegetable – on a scale that extends infinitely beyond the puny strength of the angry individual or the angry tribe.

While he is still intoxicated by this power man does not care to be reminded of the primitive beginnings from which he is still in flight. He is scornful of human ways of living which do not start from the mastery of the intellect, and his repressed longings for the spontaneity, the sexual freedom and tribal closeness of primitive man, make him all the more eager to deny the side of his humanity which he has lost.

He is only likely to change when he has doubts – doubts about the inflation he senses within himself as he tries to live up to the power he has acquired, doubts about whether, in spite of all the effort and all the denial of powerful longings, he enjoys the happiness he longs for. There is then a strong likelihood of change, but in what direction? The unconscious, which plays so powerful a part in the life of primitive man, is again insisting that it be noticed since man is paying too heavy a price for his one-sidedness, his excessive consciousness.

This change which the unconscious forces upon him may take two courses. It may lead him upon a journey of self-awareness in which he rediscovers the power of the primitive man within him and learns to integrate him with the conscious self. This is the journey which, supremely, analysis is about, but which is also open to those who, for one reason or another, cannot manage that particular route. The arts, human relationships, religion, drugs, may all make essential contributions to such a journey, though such is the two-edged nature of all that is most important to us, that any of them may also serve as an escape from the journey. Those who embark upon this journey learn a new respect for much that conscious, technological man has learned to scorn — for the hinterland of dreams, images, symbols, rituals, myths by which traditionally man charted his journey, both individually and collectively. This kind of intimate relationship with all that leads us inward — the ability to move quite naturally within the inner territory — is of the essence of the contemplative experience.

But the other kind of change which the unconscious may produce is more alarming. The man who will not embark willingly upon his journey does not escape the force of the unconscious. By one method or another it may insist upon his notice — by illness, by depression, by anxiety, by obsessions, or by collective manifestations such as sadism, racialism and war. He finds himself *taken over* by forces which he does not understand and which lead him to a conclusion that he did not want. Our over-activity, which scorns the patient travelling of the contemplative, can lead us towards such a situation, puzzled why everything we attempt turns out badly however good our intentions.

Self-awareness means trying to live with all of ourselves, the dark, injured, and furtive parts as much as the strong and respectable ones. Only thus can we avoid the 'lost' bits of our personalities acting as a kind of fifth column which sabotages all our actions.

Just as important, the kind of rhythm and self-awareness that I have been talking about leads us towards a profound and satisfying sense of the meaningfulness of life, our own life and the life that flows around us. Because we are not exhausted, because we are prepared to try to keep in touch with ourselves, then we are free at last to discover, or rediscover (we knew about it as children) the breathtaking richness of life. 'A new feeling of self-forgiveness and self-acceptance begins to spread and circulate . . . Shadow aspects of the personality continue to play their burdensome roles but now within a larger "tale", the myth of oneself, just what one is which begins to feel as if that is how one is meant to be. My myth becomes my truth; my life symbolic and allegorical . . .'[1] If we leave on one side the Jungian language in which Hillman speaks, we can still grasp the essence of his message. The journey inwards is what gives meaning to the life outside ourselves. Not in any static, dogmatic, once-for-all way either, but in a way that grows and develops and changes to meet different circumstances, different stages of development. Contem-

1. *Insearch*, James Hillman, Hodder and Stoughton.

plation is not an optional extra – it is, as much as action, part of the very stuff of being human.

The importance of contemplation to maintain our human balance is not, of course, any new discovery. Indeed, it is only because we have lost sight of something so fundamental to our well-being that it is necessary to talk of it at all. But luckily for us all there are still many ways left in which, ordinarily and unself-consciously, we lean towards the contemplative side of life.

Illness is one way known to many of us. In the first shock and frustration of illness we are annoyed at our enforced idleness and the muddle that this can create for those with whom we live or work. We feel guilty at stepping out of our ordinary duties and bored at the stillness and isolation which sickness is apt to impose upon us. Only at first, however. As the days go by we adjust ourselves to a slower rhythm and find, to our astonishment, that we are enjoying it. Our sense of guilt fades, and we realise that our practical tasks were much less urgent than we had told ourselves; anyhow, others seem to adjust to life without us rather better than we had expected, or perhaps even to enjoy the responsibility with which we have endowed them. (They may take it out on us later, of course.) Gradually we find ourselves seeing life with new eyes, noticing beauties about the world around us, sorting out longstanding problems inside ourselves, relishing tastes and colours, books and television programmes more than usual. We may find ourselves reminded of the way in which we saw life when we were children. Of course, it cannot last. We get well, our pendulum swings back towards action again, and not very willingly, perhaps with actual fear, we take up our old tasks. But the world does not look the same for a while, and we often find that we can trace later decisions and insights to these days taken unexpectedly from the earnest business of earning a living.

Weekends and holidays are another of the incidental ways in which we know about the contemplative experience. The ancestral wisdom which saw the need for a Sabbath or Sunday or other holy-day had grasped the essentially rhythmic nature of man, and his need to swing between idleness and industry. In our own day there is something of a rejection of this idea, and a movement, which sorts oddly with the spread of automation, for many people to do two jobs so that they may earn money seven days a week.

Perhaps the need to overwork becomes more insistent because we do not often recognise publicly that there are particular difficulties about weekends and holidays. Everybody is expected to enjoy them, and there is shame in admitting that one has failed to do so, and yet there is perhaps more mental pain experienced by ordinary, healthy men and women at such times than at any other. The anaesthetic of the work routine is withdrawn and various kinds of pain are felt; for example, worries about work and success may become more prominent than they are during the week, and marital problems, sexual problems, problems of dealing with children or other relatives, depressive problems, may nag us much more acutely at such times. Even physically the break from work does not at once appear to serve us well. Headache and tension, digestive and sleeping problems have a way of appearing.

These things can also, of course, be read as signs that the break from work is succeeding. We are getting the chance to know ourselves and those who are close to us, and though at first this is a shock, as with the experience of illness, we can find ourselves grateful for it. We go downward into ourselves and our problems and find that, in the end, it is not as frightful as we feared. We lose the tension and the headache, we find we can relax physically, and that we can sleep better.

Pregnancy can, for women, also be an opportunity for this incidental kind of contemplation. As with illness we find ourselves in a state where less is expected of us, and the glandular changes of pregnancy, and the sheer weight of the burden carried, encourage a slowing-down, and a less active approach to life. Carrying the unborn child also encourages a turning inward, a concentration upon the processes within, and helps us to see that we are part of a much greater whole that works in and through us.

Old age also belongs to the incidental experience of contemplation, and those of us who are not yet old can learn about contemplation from elderly relatives and friends. It is the essentially contemplative experience of life that the very old share with the very young and which so often forms such a powerful bond between them. The old have the ability to sit still, and with this often goes things which the young (and others) value; the time to chat, to listen, to tell stories of the past, to indulge in pastimes which are not strikingly useful, to play games. The fierce urgency which marks our middle years has faded in the old and there is a new sense of time. The interminable summer afternoons which we remember from early childhood seem to return, together with the special mixture of slowness, near-boredom, relish of small unremarkable moments and experiences. This makes it sound too idyllic, of course. Old age and contemplation alike have idyllic moments, but they also share the loneliness which is inescapable in either condition. It is man's condition when the drugs of busyness are removed.

Another of the ways in which we know incidentally about contemplation is through the artists. I am not to begin with speaking of the practising artist, who usually has some idea, implicit or explicit, that he is practising a form of contemplation, but of those of us who use the arts, in whatever form, to gain added pleasure and satisfaction from life.

In order to enjoy any form of art we have to discipline ourselves to stillness and attention – as with a prince, we must let it speak to us first. The discipline can be real enough, especially in all the strains and stresses of everyday life – it can feel an eccentricity to settle one's tired body and mind down to pay attention to Shakespeare or Beethoven or an exhibition or an opera. But those who are addicts of such experiences know, as by a kind of faith, what they are about. However wearily and unwillingly they go they find themselves caught up, transformed by something outside themselves, which, without taking account of their particular problems, yet speaks to their universal condition. It speaks in at least two different ways: 'It is the function of the creative individual not only to represent the highest transpersonal values of his culture, thereby becoming the honoured spokesman of his age, but also to give shape to the compensatory values and contents of which it is unconscious.'[2] When we are spectators of the arts we may be moved, therefore, either because the artist utters some consciously held belief of ourselves and our society, or because he utters that which we do not yet know that we feel and think. The second effect can either move and delight us or it can anger us.

By representing the values that are compensatory but in opposition to the cultural canon of his time he [the artist] . . . has often enough to suffer the fate of a scapegoat. For the historian, however, grasping the whole process in retrospect, the revolutionary and heretic, whether it be a Hebrew prophet or Socrates, Joan of Arc or Galileo, is as much a part of his culture as the representatives of the cultural canon who condemned him.[3]

Together they make up a whole – the inside and the outside, the conventional and the unconventional.

The artist speaks to us at an archetypal level, and at once our weariness and frustration drop away from us. We discover that we are not merely watching a play or looking at a picture which shows one particular human situation or one particular object but that we are at the centre of life itself, for 'every archetype is an aspect of the whole world and not just a fragment of it'. Erich Neumann describes this marvellous gift which genius bestows upon us

2. *The Archetypal World of Henry Moore*, Erich Neumann, tr. R. F. C. Hull, Routledge and Kegan Paul.
3. Ibid.

in the case of a painter like Rembrandt. 'Even in the smallest sketch – of a beggar, for instance – he formulates the problems of the whole world and its need of redemption, and at the same time bathes it in a mysterious redeeming light that plays over all.'[4] The genius offers us a transformed world – the world that we know and see every day of our lives in a state of transfiguration.

And here we are plunged at once into the very heart of the contemplative experience. We discipline ourselves to the point where we know something of the quality of what we witness, we pay attention, we endure the moments of loneliness and boredom, and then, sooner or later, we receive the gift of seeing our world unified and transformed. The artist himself perhaps undertakes something more sacrificial, a 'cleansing of the doors of perception', a giving of himself up to his vision.

It is striking that, in a period which values activity so much, and in which we are so suspicious of overt contemplative practices, as for instance in the case of prayer, we set so much store by the arts. The readiness to think well of the arts, and even of their most cranky and dubious exponents, reaches absurd proportions – we are as credulous in this area, as delighted to be impressed and hoodwinked and robbed, as medieval man was when confronted by miracles and relics. Nor has this epidemic probably reached its height. As mass education gives more people the training with which it is possible to enjoy the arts, and as mass media like television imprint enthusiasm for the arts as a new kind of orthodoxy, then the artists will inevitably

4. *Art and the Creative Unconscious*, Erich Neumann, Routledge and Kegan Paul.

become something of a priestly class, with scores of acolytes who '*want* to paint/write/act/dance' but who have an imperfect grasp of the intense disciplines needed to succeed even on a fairly trite level.

Within this new orthodoxy we can detect, I believe, signs of longing for the contemplative sides of life which are otherwise denied to us. We know that we need mystery and that mystery is present in the arts in a form more accessible, at least to our generation, than the mystery of religion. It is not altogether clear yet how much art may, in turn, depend upon a religious view of life, not of a dogmatic or ecclesiastical kind, but of a kind which recognises a certain order that upholds the artist and the mystery which he describes. Without some sense of order, of a 'journey' to be undertaken, the artist may lack the courage to enter the archetypal world, or when he enters it he may be too successfully seduced by its siren voices to return to us.

The courage of individual men has, however, shown itself proof against inertia, and well able to plough the tired soil of traditional religion in such a way that new life can grow. The temptations of becoming part of orthodoxy may become a greater problem. Representing orthodoxy exposes men to the perpetual temptations of any priestly class – complacency, corruption, laziness, rigidity, and a determination to maintain the status quo. And worse than any of these, inflation of personal pride to the point where any real vision becomes impossible. The flattery and high material rewards to which successful artists in our society are exposed also encourages this sort of priestly pride, and artists are no more immune than the clergy used to be to the subtle corruptions of being treated as super-beings.

Yet whatever the temptations there are always those who withstand them, who can endure the fluidity of life without trying to dam it up or imprison it for their own use. This requires a movement towards something which begins to look extraordinarily like the traditional idea of holiness. For example, a considerable amount of freedom from covetousness and ambition, a certain carelessness about material reward, a freedom to become aware of what is going on within other people, and an ability to respond to it, some discipline of desire, and above all, a lack of fear, since it is fear that makes us rigid.

Such people move naturally towards the kind of wholeness which they, and we, need, and when they are artists we can see and value their insights about the journey in their art. If they have succeeded in their art then their interest in themselves and their own 'image' wanes, as they 'give themselves up' without remainder to the ever-increasing demands of their art. The sonnets of the ageing Michelangelo movingly illustrate the state of the supreme artist at the end of his career, lustrated, humbled, acutely aware of pain and gratefully aware of joy, free to see what is before his eyes.

A New Approach to Contemplation

If we sense, tentatively, that there is something in the art of contemplation that we have to explore for ourselves, then we are ready to experiment with its possibilities in different areas of our lives. It demands caution, since we are not talking about some passing fad but about one of the deep springs of human life; if we get it wrong, or cause others to get it wrong, then we are muddying the drinking pool. It is not something to be taken up for our own gratification, like a drawing-room trick, nor even is it primarily to be undertaken for our deepest fulfilment. It is more like a beautiful and valuable stone which we want to take into our hand from time to time, enjoying holding it and looking at it in various lights and moods, content to let it give us whatever it can.

In any case, it is going to be difficult. In a society that is orientated towards speed, activity, productivity, material ambition, success, and sensation, then those who insist on other goals are not going to be very popular. In fact, they could easily be seen as saboteurs, undermining the consumer-society we have carefully built up (which depends for its continuance on a high degree of discontent and the waste which this encourages). Yet it is important that we should not just exchange one unbalanced view of life for another. If we react too strongly against activity, despising all that it has achieved and hopes to achieve, then we are denying the rhythm which I believe to be the essentially human condition which transcends both action and contemplation. The beatniks, hippies, and the sort of drug cultists who glorify contemplation above all else are missing the essential humanness of their lives as much as the busiest bishop or tycoon. The pendulum is not to be held at one end of the swing or the other.

Man needs activity to control his environment. He needs it to provide himself with food and shelter, to save himself from being destroyed by animal or insect life or by disease, and to distribute the assets of his society in a way that shares the opportunities of physical and mental development as widely as possible. He needs activity to cultivate his intellect, his feelings and emotions, his desires and appetites. It is the voice of change. Seen over against activity, contemplation can easily be represented as the slide into laziness, inefficiency, corruption and squalor of which the active are so deeply afraid.

What has contemplation got to offer by way of an equal claim to human happiness and well-being? Contemplation is the way of feeling at home in one's environment, of letting oneself off the need to fight it all the time, and permitting oneself to enjoy it. It is the voice of conservation, relishing what is already known and asking only to be allowed to know it in greater detail and in greater depth. It is concerned with depth, with growth, with meaning on an almost wordless level; it touches upon the deep springs of the individual and of society.

Action and contemplation only become dynamic in so far as each interacts with the other. If action stands for the 'ego' of man, contemplation stands for his unconscious, and both are needed to make up the whole man. The active side of man needs the contemplative side to resolve the deep questions about aims and meanings, and the direction which action ought to take. Otherwise it will merely become fussy and futile, performing useless rituals that have become unbreakable habits, the joy and the sense of purpose swiftly ebbing away. Art will become rubbishy and sterile, religion will lose all its vitality, relationships will be shallow and timid, material satisfactions and the more superficial kinds of sexual satisfaction will occupy a more and more important place. Without contemplation man ceases to feel himself *rooted*, and without roots there can be no stillness, no security, and no growth. Change sweeps away all that is recognisable, reassuring and meaningful.

Way of Life

I would like to look at what I think it could mean for a twentieth-century man to learn to value the contemplative side of himself as well as the active side. He is lucky in that a more contemplative approach to life is not far behind him in his history; he can still reach back to it in memory by recalling life in his grandparents' home, or the quality of life in Britain until a generation or so ago (and to some extent in some remote places it has still preserved its old quality). In another generation there may be no first-hand experience of the quality of life I am talking about unless we can, without quaintness or crankiness, capture something of that same quality in our own lives.

It is not easy to talk of changing the quality of life without allowing a fatal self-consciousness to creep into the discussion. Inevitably we turn to particular models either in the past or the present; we try to absorb their virtues as by a kind of osmosis, and until we have grown tired of them we find it difficult to notice their vices as well. If we seek our models in the present we may look to a particular group which spells freedom from the conventions. If we wish to identify with them we may grow our hair or our beards, wear a certain style of clothes, eat certain kinds of food, frequent particular places. If we do so we may find ourselves drawn into the group and discover that there are certain things that it can give us, certain things that it cannot give us. What it may give us is courage to change, and this is no slight gift; the drawback, however, will be that we will get caught into a form of inclusiveness (of a sort of which the Church in history offers a telling example) which probably produces a good deal of paranoia about those outside the group which in turn is countered with a feeling of superiority towards them.

Suppose, however, we take our models from further back in history. We remember, or have been told about, a more secure way of life (secure in the sense of being un-likely to change very fast) in which the warmth of family and village and town life had not yet given way to the vast impersonality of commuterdom, the housing estate and the supermarket. According to our political stance we will shuffle arguments about the desirability or otherwise of the change, recalling on the one hand the golden serenity of Edwardian England (for those who lived above the bread line), and on the other the terrible exploitation of the poor and uneducated which accompanied it.

Such attempts at finding models bewilder us by the complexity of the evidence; we would like to be part of a new, liberating movement, but are cynical about its chances of escaping corruption. We think wistfully of certain aspects of the past, but cannot stomach the par-ticular brand of brutality which we know underlay it.

I believe, however, that with a more conscious aware-ness of what we do, we might learn how to select those aspects of the past or the present which we need without becoming wholly subject to them. It is possible to take up and enjoy current tastes, fashions and enthusiasms without becoming slavishly 'trendy', provided we can take pleasure in the things for their own sake and not as a passport to some 'in' group which will bolster up our self-doubt. It is possible, too, to be open with the right sort of humility to the insights of the past that we have lost or overlaid, in fact it is the only way to keep ourselves fully aware of all the potentialities of our humanness.

Given this sort of flexibility we can return to the attempt to evolve a way of life for ourselves which gives proper weight to both active and contemplative sides of our personality. We need not fear that we shall be too impressed by any of our models (nor suffer the subsequent disillusion when we see that we hoped for too much). And we can perhaps save ourselves from moving towards an ever more joyless fate, losing as we go the most precious possession of human beings – the *expectation* of joy. Contemplation is essentially a state that *expects* joy, which perhaps is why it can enter the darkest experiences of being human and emerge unscathed.

If we have some sense of the rhythmic quality of life then we can, at least in maturity, avoid the wilder extremes. We need neither race headlong after money and position and fame nor feel that it is somehow more blessed to live on a shoestring. We are creatures who need our occasional triumphs, windfalls, treats and extravagances if we are not to lose heart altogether, yet if we have too much then our appetite quickly becomes blunted and we become blasé about the simpler delights, and begin to think the world revolves around our whims and moods.

The first step in admitting the contemplative element in our lives may lie in an assessment of how much money we need to lead the kind of life which we and our families find tolerable, and what this means in terms of sacrifice for the breadwinner and others. Breadwinning easily becomes a slavery with men trapped in jobs they detest for a whole life-time. An excessive dread of loss of security makes cowards of us, a cowardice which friends and relatives encourage with reminders of responsibility. But perhaps the vast majority of breadwinners in a society like ours could afford to be much more daring than they are, considering the possibility of taking several months off between jobs in which to think, read, work with their hands. I have known a few people who have actually saved up, over a period of years, for the privilege of a spell of this sort of idleness.

Some professional and industrial jobs actually allow a sabbatical, but those who are not so lucky have to set about arranging it for themselves. In a society so obsessed with status as ours, many middle-class people have riddled themselves with crippling expenses that make any break difficult; it is worth considering the kind of bondage in which we place ourselves when we invest in expensive houses with fashionable addresses, costly educational plans for our children, the habit of expensive holidays, cars, household equipment, and all the costly toys with which the advertisements tempt us. But it is easier to make a break than we suppose before we have the courage to do it. It matters surprisingly little if our car grows old, our house gets shabby and our overdraft gets large. Relative poverty of this sort, though irritating, is much less alarming than we imagined when caught up in a more expensive way of life. It can be a small price to pay for the precious sense of inner liberty, of freedom to grow and to be.

We need not suppose that we shall be in this state of

withdrawal for the rest of our lives. Although, when worn out with activity, it is difficult for us to believe that we shall ever really choose to exert ourselves again, nevertheless, after an unhurried period of contemplation, we shall once again be ready for activity. Refreshed by rest, and re-orientated by the chance to go deeply into ourselves, we shall find to our astonishment that what once seemed such a burden to us now comes easily, and that where previously we had felt our courage and vision and hope ebbing away, we have recovered confidence and direction.

I hope we are coming to a time in which more people have the courage to make this sort of break. At the moment we are still circulating propaganda to the effect that a life-time of unbroken work (often to the point of breakdown and beyond) constitutes virtue, and it is tragic to note that those who have the best chance of observing at first hand the damage this does to individuals and to society – doctors, analysts, clergy, social workers – are often the most fanatical in overworking. If we can be more critical of the propaganda in favour of work to which we are all exposed from infancy onwards, then perhaps it may be possible to convince them that far from being evidence of their faithfulness and devotion to others, it is, on the contrary, a gross betrayal of those they serve and of all who are working towards a better quality of life.

The megalomania which allows us to believe that life cannot go on unless we, personally, work ourselves beyond our modest strength is a pathological state which must be fought, in ourselves, our friends, and our nearest and dearest. Sanity returns as our exhausted minds and bodies are allowed to rest, and when they have rested they discover more important and life-giving goals than productivity, or our own professional reputation, or an expensive style of life.

The kind of long break I am talking about may not be needed very often – perhaps no more than twice or three times in a working life, and usually at times of re-orientation. At the end of schooling or university is often one such period of re-orientation, when the chance of leisure, and perhaps of travel, may be of crucial importance in helping to work out the future, particularly so far as work is concerned, but perhaps also as far as emotional relationships are concerned. The next 'natural break' seems to occur in middle-life, just before or just after forty. A man or woman's life-style is by then fully established, both as regards work and family, yet the needs of the family are no longer quite as demanding as they were at an earlier stage. No other 'break' is quite so obvious as these two, except possibly the break which may come at the beginning of retirement, yet there may be many situations, of crisis or otherwise, which for the individual signal a new kind of life which demands a period of preparation. The completion of a long and difficult piece of work, the giving up of a particular job, a bereavement, or even some unexpected insight about oneself, may suddenly make the need for withdrawal imperative, and save one a later, involuntary withdrawal caused by illness.

An interesting question is what form these sabbaticals should take. When we are in an exhausted state we find it impossible to imagine 'letting go' completely, and out of our tiredness we make elaborate plans for ourselves – plans of a different sort of work, of books to read, tasks to get done, long-cherished hobbies to take up. Ideally, I believe, we should only use these to help ourselves into a 'running down' process, in which we try to do less and less until the moment when we can do nothing at all and face the fact with equanimity. We may take weeks to get to this point, weeks in which we struggle with guilt at our 'laziness', and with a growing sense of depression and self-dissatisfaction. If we can persist with this then we reach a sort of nub or core of the experience. Our depression becomes very great, there is a strong sense of pain and darkness, and we find ourselves gazing down into the deep springs of our personalities, and of life itself. Once we have reached this still point, and have rested at it, however briefly, then we begin to move, slowly at first, back towards activity. It is not difficult to be slow – we have learned how absurd it is to hurry in the way we usually do – and one by one we can again pick up the tasks that interest us, and which seem proper to our development, finding that we see them with new eyes. We have a new vision about ourselves and our lives.

The kind of 'running down' I have described is not easy for most people. It runs counter to the rooted British horror of 'introspection', and it touches upon the deep fears which most of us have concerning what goes on inside us. It follows that circumstances can help or hinder a good deal. The most important ingredient of the sort of withdrawal I am describing is long periods of being alone, whether this happens at home or elsewhere. But certain stages may need to be done away from home. Uncomprehending relatives can be unsympathetic to the need for loneliness or silence, and with children it can be impossible. Convents and monasteries, particularly of the contemplative kind, can be very supportive for short periods, and especially periods of crisis. Lay communities, like that of St. Julians, understand a lot about giving the undisturbed quiet and absence of responsibility which make it possible to concentrate on inner struggles. For longer-term sabbaticals a stay in a country district, particularly a fairly remote one where the inhabitants have a close sense of relationship to one another can, as it were, jerk the needle out of the groove where we usually get stuck. But there's no need to be too folksy about it. For some people cities can give the kind of anonymity that is life-giving. For others some kind of group or community which will take them very positively into its life for a while is what is needed. Perhaps there needs to be an element of daring in the way a sabbatical is spent – we need to have the courage for something which both frightens and attracts us. When it is over we need not just to feel more energetic, but as if we have achieved something at a personal level.

Shorter breaks

Just as a life-time needs to be broken by one or two long periods of withdrawal, so our ordinary working life needs to be punctuated by shorter breaks. In these we can go less deeply, but deeply enough to preserve a sense of the importance of the contemplative principle in our lives. The long weekend, a week or so away from the family, even the day spent alone and more or less in silence (some experiences like listening to music can deepen the silence) can all serve to this end.

It can mean a lot to know of somewhere where we can go to find the peace we are looking for, somewhere where stillness and the contemplative principle is taken for granted.

The contemplative principle can touch upon the tiniest details of our working life – upon whether we allow ourselves a break at lunchtime, or feel guilty if we just sit and chat to a friend or watch television. Can we sit still? This is the really important question. Or must we be always yielding to our obsessions and getting up to tidy up, or pandering to our inflated self-importance by pretending that we can never stop working.

I am not talking about laziness. There is a kind of laziness, often closely related to depression, in which it is too much bother to make any effort, hours drift by with little to show for them, and fruitless chatter with people we don't much like can waste whole hours. Contemplation is not laziness – there is tension in it – though it is nearer to laziness than to bustling activity. It isn't what is called 'letting yourself go' – a pathetic collapse into physical squalor and mental idleness. But it is 'letting go', letting go of some of the anxieties and fears and longings which strain and bewilder us. It is not motivated by fear, as laziness is – fear of trying to live at all in case one fails. On the contrary it is motivated by a wish to get to grips with life and a realisation that this can only be done if there is time and space to look inside ourselves.

Relationships

At first sight the contemplative principle seems inimical to relationship. Activity plays such a crucial part in meeting and getting to know people, for maintaining friendships with them, or, in the case of a sexual relationship, of making love, that it seems to exclude any contemplative considerations. And we tend to think of contemplation in terms of man struggling with profound insights of his own.

Yet I believe that nowhere is contemplation of more importance than in the matter of relationship. The heart of contemplation lies in a sense of 'thereness' and it is often in our lack of a sense of thereness either of ourself or others that our relationship problems begin. We may have difficulty in perceiving ourselves as a real person in the eyes of others, or feel that it is only by clinging desperately to the love and affection of others that we can have any life at all. We may lack a sense of our own value, our own 'richness', and be eaten up with envy for all that others have by way of looks, or success, or money or possessions, or happiness. We may feel ourselves dominated or devoured by others – our relatives or employers. We may feel put upon. We may be persecuted by our fantasies of the life we would have liked, or the satisfactions which we need and long for.

I don't want to suggest that contemplation is, or should be, the cure for these things, or that that is its function, and yet it does enter, in an important way, into all these problems. Partly because it stands for detachment. To detach ourselves, however temporarily and partially, from the heat of our desires and hopes and disappointments, gives us some perspective in an area of our lives where perspective is needed. Trying to relax into ourselves in the ways I have described can make us aware, whatever the personality problems with which we are cursed, that however unlikely it feels at times, it really is us there standing on that particular spot and no one else. We can begin to inhabit ourselves, to have faith in the fact that we are this person, whatever the drawbacks, and no other, and that it is *this* life that is there to be lived. Some of the sense of poverty leaves us and with it the envy which can make life such a torture, or the insatiable appetite which reduces us to a state of perpetual starvation. An unexpected strength flows out of this new-found 'thereness'. Not the old kind of strength in which we drove ourselves on, against the grain, to do things we didn't want to do, but a new kind of strength which allows us to admit our weakness to ourselves, and sometimes to others, and live with the weakness of being human, not a superman. This love for the humanity in ourselves and others is perhaps the most costly and humiliating thing we ever have to undertake. We discover that we are 'just human', not saints, not gods, not angels, not devils, not unusual, not special, not 'good men', or even bad men. Progress is to grow in respect for 'ordinariness' and to learn to live it gladly, accepting our weakness and failure just as much as our strength and triumph. It is the road to wholeness.

The ordinariness, despite its costliness, is disappointingly undramatic, and is a blow to the exhibitionist side of us which would love to figure in some more flattering role. Its value, however, lies in its reality. It is only interested in things as they are, not as they would be if we lived up to our idealised picture of ourselves, not as they may be at some future date. It is the reflection in the mirror before we have put on our best expression, or the photograph of us which was taken unawares.

But the reality of it is what makes relationship possible. When we are not acting, then we do not force others to act either, to take part in our private little charades. Our honesty, simplicity, and lack of guile give them the opportunity for an equally straightforward response. They become real, not part of our fantasy.

It would be foolish to pretend that we always have a choice about these things. Certain pathological states, and certain situations, enforce acting upon us as the only way of preserving our inner self from intolerable pain or destruction. But contemplation, because it is about being, makes it easier to resist that kind of seduction, easier to discover that we have a self whom we can be.

This is nowhere more important than in our sexual relationships where the problem of integrating the self, or bringing our desire and our feeling together can be a very real one. The disintegrating effect for the individual, and for those whom he 'loves', of allowing sexual appetite to be split off from any real sense of the partner as a person, is well known. Both the partners become anonymous, and are forced to accept an injury to their 'being' side. Promiscuity is, in fact, activity taken to the uttermost limit, action finally cut off from its root of 'being'.

The great and painful effort at integration for the sexually promiscuous lies in developing their being side, partly by living in their fantasies instead of acting them out, partly by attempting the frightening feat of bringing desire and love together, of making love where they do, in fact, love. This touches upon emotional injuries of longstanding which it is painful to acknowledge and seek a cure for.

For others the problem is almost the opposite one. They can banish sexual desire from their lives all too easily, and are mystified at the huge part it plays in the way others think and feel. They are sealed, virginal, in their thoughts and feelings, and may, at worst, feel superior to the suffering and struggles of others where sexual feeling is concerned. Compared to the promiscuous, they are invulnerable; they never court the rebuffs, disappointments, humiliation and ruin which is the lot of the sexually adventurous. Yet it is their invulnerability that prohibits growth. They dread the torrents of feeling that sex can release; without, as a rule, knowing it, they cannot take the risk of abandoning themselves to experience, of 'letting go'. Ecstasy, the 'panic' which the Greek god Pan used to inflict on unwary maidens, is the madness they fear above all others. But ecstasy is the knowledge of 'being', one's own being and the being of the world about one, and not infrequently accompanies contemplative states. No one can become contemplative without leaving room for the irruption of ecstasy into their life, and the knowledge of its primacy when it does irrupt. Those damaged on this side of their personality have as difficult a journey as the promiscuous.

Such sexual problems are deeply and inextricably involved with relationship problems, and these are often most painfully experienced within marriage and the family. So profound is our society's reverence for the family that we are all the victims of propaganda which almost invariably presents marriage and child-rearing as an infallibly happy process. We have only to look about us, to listen to our friends and colleagues, to read books, to know that the

truth can be very different. The best arguments in favour
of marriage and family life are not that they promote
happiness and reduce loneliness, though at their best they
do these things, but that they create a situation in which
facing the truth about ourselves – our self-deceiving,
touchy, vain, inflated selves – becomes more difficult to
avoid than it is anywhere else. Even in marriage, and even
as parents, human beings *do* manage to evade the truth for
long periods, at appalling cost to everyone concerned, but
it is harder to do than in most other human situations.
And seeing the truth is always accompanied by pain and
humiliation. No marriage and no family which rigidly
excludes pain is likely to be doing its job, and most families
will avoid pain if they can. The sort of marriage where the
couple never have a row, cannot bear 'unpleasantness', the
sort of family that is endlessly and determinedly 'happy'
cannot lead to growth, nor any genuine form of 'being'.
'Being' is about acknowledging one's pain, and not trying
to conceal it from oneself, or inflict it upon others. For
most of us there is a lot of pain inside to be acknowledged
– anxiety, doubts of our own worth, moods of sadness and
gloom and failure. The temptation to dodge it all by our
busyness, our success, our innumerable friends and diver-
sions, is very great.

The particular temptation of family life, the obverse of
letting it help one to see the truth about oneself, is to allow
it to become a prison, and oneself a helpless prisoner
within it. Part of us wants imprisonment and the simplicity and lack of choice which it inflicts. It is a kind of
security, notwithstanding the intense bitterness and frustration we can feel behind the bars. The humourless

rigidity of the traditional Western attitudes to love and sex have made the prison exceptionally grim and the security astonishingly impregnable. The grimness of the prison has been most evident in the kind of emotional blackmail which couples have inflicted upon one another. Perhaps the worst blackmail of all has lain in the pretence that love between two people who have met when fairly young, and have usually married for unconscious reasons with a strong neurotic content, can supply all that is needed, emotionally, intellectually, sexually – for growth over what may be a period of fifty or sixty years. Because we tend to marry young and because the expectation of life is longer than it has ever been, marriage has now become a longer term contract than it ever was before. In the case of the 'good' marriage, that is the marriage which allows growth, and in which there is, therefore, an awareness of freedom, generosity, sympathy and comfort, this is an undoubted blessing. But what of the many marriages that are prisons—the ones that stifle, deny, wound and destroy – what are they but the breeding grounds of mental and physical illness and of a new generation of neurotics?

There is no slick answer to problems as grave and tragic as these. Neither the Churches' quivering horror when anyone attacks 'the sanctity of marriage', nor the sophisticates' glib divorcing and sleeping-around begins to reach out towards the real pain and bewilderment that men and women experience in this area of their lives. It is the very unanswerableness of it all that makes the pain so great, and drives us towards rigid solutions either of a conservative or radical nature.

I believe this is a situation to which contemplation can speak. Contemplation is about waiting, if necessarily in pain, within a fixed situation which is what marriage is. It is about finding the answers that lie not without but within, about finding freedom from the inner attitudes which bind us, with a terrible compulsiveness, into one kind of slavery or another.

Forms of slavery in marriage are not far to seek. The husband bitterly bound to the responsibilities of making money, the wife determinedly sacrificing her gifts and talents for the family, both of them bound by guilt, by what their parents thought about marriage or about life, by traditional roles of male and female, and by what the neighbours think. As slaves do, they take their pain out on one another, playing deathly games in which selfishness, anger, and hate are dressed up to look like unselfishness, patience and love.

We can only set ourselves free from such sickness by going deeply enough into ourselves to find the courage to be what we are, and it is only when we are what we are that it will be possible for our marriage partners, or anyone else, to relate properly to us. Being what we are feels perilous, as in a sense it is, since it makes us indifferent to the shallow beliefs and conventions of 'society'. We become fully prepared to make our own moral choices and to take the consequences, and this does not necessarily commend us to those who only feel safe when backed up by authority, or those who see themselves as authority. There is a loneliness in this kind of adulthood which cannot be denied, but it is the only way out of prison, and the only way to be done with our grumbling, our acting and our self-pity.

I do not believe that marriage is the only *impasse* of our time to which contemplation speaks. It is striking how many of the problems which bedevil us have the same air of utter insolubility. Conservation and pollution, the population explosion, economic problems, social problems, traffic problems are all surrounded by arguments of such extreme and unyielding complexity that attempts to deal with them realistically fill us with despair. For every argument there is a counter-argument, and beyond every solution a fresh problem. We defend ourselves with bombs against enemies who would destroy us, and find that we have released poisons which will kill our descendants if not ourselves. We attack the insect life which endangers our food and health and discover that we have taken away the livelihood of other creatures we loved and valued. We make giant strides in saving the lives of babies, of stamping out killers like tuberculosis, and of prolonging the lives of old people. And we find ourselves severely over-populated, overcrowded to the point where many are homeless, where the streets are clogged with traffic, and where the countryside is endangered.

In our despair at the complexity of the issues involved we are once again tempted towards rigid attitudes. It is so much easier to take any of these grave problems in a one-sided way, to consider it only as it affects us at this moment, because this at once leads us towards some form of action which helps us to feel that we have eliminated the problem. But the problems are too serious for one-sided ness and prejudice, or for quick forms of relief. We need to counter this temptation in ourselves by moving a little away from the problems, and trying to set them into the context of the quality of life we would like to see in this country, and we can only hope to do this if we have some real knowledge of the quality of life we are seeking within ourselves. It is as if we may no longer think in fragments — the countryside, insects, birds, animals, people, towns, motor cars, the nation, war, bombs, the moon, space — but are being forced by events to think in terms of a whole, that is of life, as it ebbs and flows around us in all its immense variety of forms. And it seems as if we can only bear to confront life as a whole when inside ourselves we are moving towards some state of wholeness of our own, a state in which we know in microcosm about the joy and agony of the world.

Contemplation seems to speak to our condition, or at least to offer a fruitful approach to our problems. We have travelled so far from the natural rhythms of nature that we scarcely remember what they were — we no longer wake at sunrise nor reduce our activity in the winter, and we are not, except by a conscious effort, aware of the position of the sun and stars, or even acutely aware of the seasons. We have lost that natural rootedness, and with it has gone something spontaneous and uncalculating in our relations with one another, precious forms of inner certainty about ourselves, and about the existence of what men have called God.

What may be the most important attitude in our time is that we have at last begun to feel a sense of loss. The complacency of the Victorians, still firmly believing in God and progress and the British Empire, is not for us. We have seen too much suffering to believe in nationalism, or imperialism, or progress, or the essential goodness of man. The long years of triumph for European civilisation have been followed by years of bitter pain and self-criticism. We see a melancholy future ahead of us – a future of over-crowding, of pollution, of disastrous war, of racial conflict, of stress diseases and of galloping neurosis.

It is the scale and gravity of the problems which con-stitutes our greatest hope since it makes it possible to believe that we can be shaken out of our lethargy, our prejudice, our certainty that 'things will work out all right' and forced to a new evaluation of what our lives are about.

No fruitful action is likely to emerge unless, slowly and painstakingly, we make such an evaluation first, and I be-lieve that we cannot make such an evaluation without moving towards the dark, contemplative side of human experience, with its long tradition of stillness, silence, patience and loneliness. For many of us it, and the new approach to life and people which follow it, may be the only contribution we can make towards healing a sick society.

With the help of this approach we can refuse to let ourselves be stampeded by busyness, tempted by excessive materialism, or drugged by activity. Equally we can refuse authoritarianism in whatever form it seduces us – political or religious, and we can insist on looking behind and be-neath the conventional texts and platitudes and slogans in order to find a truth which really lives for us and for our contemporaries. We mustn't let ourselves be deceived by fools, however highly placed, who care less for humanity than for their own success.

The most difficult and worthwhile feat of all is to become so rich inside ourselves that we become careless of other forms of wealth and status. This richness, and the stillness out of which it comes, really makes it possible to love others. Our children, our marriage partner, our colleague, our friends, are no longer any kind of threat, and can therefore be given the undivided attention, the absolute concentration, which is only possible in freedom.

For some people the way to move towards this state is by prayer, for others the necessary nourishment comes by way of aesthetic experience, sexual ecstasy, love of people or of God; perhaps more people than we are yet ready to admit need of all these things as ingredients of inner growth and might have them if we were not so rigid with fear and bewildered by the drugs which anaesthetise fear.

Of course, it is difficult and painful and of course, we may not get very far. But even to move in this direction, even to admit it as a legitimate effort, or a legitimate topic of conversation, can change our thinking and the thinking of our children. Not that it is a revolution. It is merely the recognition of something we have known all along about ourselves; that we are contemplatives.